D0119493

Must I Repeat Myself . . .?

Must I Repeat Myself . . .?

Unpublished Letters to
𝕿𝖍𝖊 𝕯𝖆𝖎𝖑𝖞 𝕿𝖊𝖑𝖊𝖌𝖗𝖆𝖕𝖍

EDITED BY

IAIN HOLLINGSHEAD WITH KATE MOORE

**WHITE
LION**
PUBLISHING

Brimming with creative inspiration, how-to projects and useful
information to enrich your everyday life, Quarto Knows is a favourite
destination for those pursuing their interests and passions. Visit our
site and dig deeper with our books into your area of interest:
Quarto Creates, Quarto Cooks, Quarto Homes, Quarto Lives,
Quarto Drives, Quarto Explores, Quarto Gifts, or Quarto Kids.

First published in 2018 by White Lion Publishing
an imprint of The Quarto Group
The Old Brewery, 6 Blundell Street
London N7 9BH
United Kingdom

www.QuartoKnows.com

ISBN 978 1 78131 796 9

10 9 8 7 6 5 4 3 2 1

2022 2021 2020 2019 2018

Typeset in Mrs Eaves by SX Composing DTP, Rayleigh, Essex
Printed by CPI Group (UK) Ltd, Croydon, CR0 4YY

MIX
Paper from
responsible sources
FSC® C020471
www.fsc.org

SIR — There are three reasons why I subscribe to *The Daily Telegraph*: the crossword, Matt and the prospect of seeing a letter published.

I guess two out of three ain't bad.

Andy Dabson
Liss, Hampshire

SIR — As so many people are apologising, it is clearly the thing to do, so I apologise too. Apologies for writing.

Hugo Summerson
London SW20

CONTENTS

CONTENTS

INTRODUCTION

Happy birthday to the unpublished letters series! Over the course of 10 books and more than 5,000 letters, some of which featured on *Have I Got News for You* (during the MPs' expenses scandal) and the *Today* programme (in a debate about why more men write than women), the readers have passed caustic comment on three Prime Ministers; two referenda; three American Presidents; the wives (and mistresses) of three French Presidents; one Russian leader (whether he called himself President or Prime Minister); two Royal weddings (three if, like the Picture Editor, you consider Pippa Middleton part of the family); three Royal births; two Summer Olympic Games; three World Cups; six series of *Downton Abbey*; numerous mispronunciations, misprints and marital misunderstandings; and just one Silvio Berlusconi.

Time flies when the letter-writers are having fun.

Looking through the previous editions, it struck me how much has changed. The readers have watched London burn, the Middle East revolt, Prince William grow bald, Prince Harry grow up and England get slightly better at football, losing twice to Belgium, instead of once to Iceland. They have bade fond and furious farewells, sometimes more than once, to everyone from Tony Blair to Osama bin Laden, Louise Mensch to Ed Miliband. Scandals came and went, including Bunga Bunga, *Top Gear*, horse lasagne, Cecil Rhodes, Rolf Harris, phone-tapping and super-injunctions ("a morning-after pill for celebrities?" suggested one reader). I particularly enjoyed revisiting the letters from "M", the correspondent who believed himself (at least, I always assumed it was a he) the head of MI5, writing from an internet café in Bristol. Sadly, he appears to have gone even deeper undercover (to the West Country, perhaps, beyond the reach of superfast broadband) since the sixth edition. We have missed his musings on whether Tom Daley is a CIA spy or Cherie Blair the secret leader of ISIS.

Most of all, however, there is a sense of continuity across the series. As one correspondent, who had also recently re-read all nine books, points out this year, the names of the targets might change, but the rants remain as eclectic and humorous as ever. Readers still grapple with modern media, manners and technology (Alexa and driverless cars are new entries in the latter category this year). They're still wonderfully willing to share the intimacies of their domestic lives with a wide audience. And, you might notice, many of them continue to be more than mildly miffed about the EU. Mrs May's Chequers deal in July this year prompted a heavier postbag than any event since the duck houses and home-flipping of 2009.

While the news cycle can, at times, appear painfully repetitive, *Telegraph* letter-writers can always be relied upon, therefore, to provide an original angle. This anniversary year finds them on especially good form, whether wondering if Meghan Markle has ever visited Sussex; reminiscing about how to wield a hatpin in the days before #MeToo; or coping with heatwaves and snow storms, sometimes in the same month.

I am particularly tickled by their enduring ability to relate items in the news to their own lives — and vice versa. Donald Trump tweets his latest banality; grandparents write about how the President reminds them of their young, irrational grandchildren. The Russians interfere with other countries' politics; a reader wonders if his online grocery order has also been hacked. Drugs testing is introduced across more sports; perhaps pension advisers should be tested in a similar way? A British-made food-processor blade leaps out of a European dishwasher without a second glance — is there a Brexit parallel there?

It is sad for me to reflect, therefore, that this is my final year at the editor's helm. Like Jeremy Clarkson, Chris Huhne and Colonel Gaddafi — albeit for happier reasons — it is time to move on. Although I won't miss the attempts at poetry (the numerous versions of "To Leave or not to Leave" were especially painful last year), there is a huge amount which I will look back fondly on (sorry, readers — *upon which* I will look back fondly). I will never forget our correspondents' gentle, but lethal, ability to prick pomposity in all its forms; their desire to grow old disgracefully (and sexily); their gloriously unhealthy relationship with alcohol; or their bewildered determination to understand a world that has sometimes changed quicker than they might have hoped. As well as their wit, erudition and occasional downright lunacy, I have especially enjoyed their historical perspective — reminiscing, for example, about burying grand pianos in their gardens in the 1950s or comparing this summer's heatwave with the drought of 1976. I have also been hugely appreciative of their great personal warmth; many have made regular appearances in my own inbox, as well as in the newspaper's.

Fortunately, I leave the series in the capable hands of Kate Moore, who has been invaluable in helping to compile the last three editions. I am grateful to her, as I am, as ever, to Christopher Howse, the Letters Editor, and the incomparable Matt, the cartoonist. I shall continue to follow the books as a reader – and, who knows, one day maybe even as a tentative letter-writer myself. For now, however, I shall enjoy leaving it to the seasoned experts. I hope the *Telegraph*'s very own – and very special – correspondents feel a little less alone than they did back in 2009.

Iain Hollingshead
London SE22

FAMILY LIFE AND
TRIBULATIONS

Testing times on the home front

SIR – My initial reaction on reading your headline "Testing four-year-olds" was: "Aren't they all?"

Garry Rucklidge
Chapel Allerton, Somerset

SIR – We are all aware of the sleep deprivation that young mothers suffer. I was therefore impressed by the wistful comment heard recently in our Community Centre: "When my two-year-old becomes a stroppy teenager I am going to wake him up at four in the morning to tell him that one of my socks has come off."

Dave Alsop
Gloucester

SIR – During the usual "career choice" sessions at school, our youngest sister, in a moment of teenaged parent-baiting, announced to her patient father that she thought prostitution might be a lucrative career.

Our darling father didn't flinch, replying that he really didn't mind what she decided to do with her life, as long as she was happy and had a good pension plan.

Susy Goodwin
Ware, Hertfordshire

SIR – My family joined me at the weekend to celebrate my birthday. We were playing some traditional party games when my six-year-old grandson jumped up and exclaimed, "This is almost fun."

I hope I live to hear him make the same comment, omitting the "almost".

Margaret Scattergood
Knowle, West Midlands

SIR – I was delighted to receive today the following letter from my ten-year-old grandson: "Thank you for my remote control car. It is really cool and it doesn't matter that it doesn't work."

Alice Cleland
Devizes, Wiltshire

SIR – Thank goodness one is not expected to write a thank-you letter to one's husband. I would definitely have struggled to write one on receiving, some years ago, a set of blue car headlamps and a twin-tone horn.

Sandra Hawke
Andover, Hampshire

SIR – My eight-year-old granddaughter may have shown a degree of prescience beyond her years when she was recently heard to say that first there is childhood, then the teenage years and finally adultery.

Mike Spragg
Great Yarmouth, Norfolk

Rubbish date

SIR – Perhaps I should forget Tinder, internet dating or more recently *Love in the Countryside*: it would seem all the men are down at the tip. The queue was 40-deep on Saturday.

Girls, you'll have to be up early though to catch these worms as it was at eight o'clock in the morning.

Ellie Withers
Hurst, Berkshire

Indecisive proposal

SIR — "Regular sex boosts the memory of over-fifties", says your headline.

I had intended to show this report to my wife. I forgot.

Nigel Hawkins
Braunton, Devon

SIR — I was born in 1930 and my only sibling, my brother, was born in 1913.

Did my mother have the longest headache known to medical science or did my father get his memory back?

Joe Hill
St Agnes, Cornwall

SIR — Scientists have found that sex and sleep are the keys to real happiness. Presumably not at the same time?

Roy Hughes
Marlbrook, Worcestershire

SIR – I note that the current birth rate is falling. Would this be connected with the relative unattractiveness of the male of the species by virtue of the mass of body paintings they now sport?

Graham Jones
Tytherington, Cheshire

Stop meeting me at McDonald's

SIR – I would be delighted if the hairstyle known as "Meet me at McDonald's" was banned, not just by schools but by the government. It would stop me having to peer at groups of lanky male youths to see which one, if any, is my nephew.

Extending the ban to the words *sweet*, *legend* and *sick* might even win my vote.

James Dixon
Stanningfield, Suffolk

SIR – Occasionally my late husband would shave off his beard at the start of a holiday so that the children and I could see what he really looked like.

Our joint opinion was always the same and, after the two-week break, he would return to work supporting a handsome and dignified growth.

Zoe Percy
Orpington, Kent

SIR – My very bald grandfather was a dignified and loyal man, but changed his barber after many years following this exchange.

Grandfather (being invited to the chair): "Shall I take my coat off?"

Barber: "You don't really need to take your hat off."

Mik Shaw
Goring-by-Sea, West Sussex

Black shoe diaries

SIR – I overheard the following exchange in a supermarket queue some years ago.

Mother to daughter: "I need some new black shoes."

Daughter: "But you've got some black shoes, Mother."

"Yes, but your Uncle Arthur's very ill."

Jacqueline Atwell
Felbridge, Surrey

SIR – If sunglasses are now being used for their intended purpose, instead of as hair bands, is it too much to hope that caps may soon start to be worn the right way round?

Russell Parkes
Penshurst, Kent

SIR – My wife is unimpressed by camouflage trousers because, as she rightly points out, they are still easily recognisable as trousers.

Eldon Sandys
Pyrford, Surrey

SIR – Why in recent years have men's trouser zips been shortened from eight inches to six inches? It is very inconvenient.

Timothy Collett
Ashtead, Surrey

Tent poles apart

SIR – Judith Woods writes in her column that, when camping with her husband, "his tent erection is as strong and stable as anything decreed by Kubla Khan". Even during our honeymoon under canvas in Scotland my own wife has never been as complimentary.

Dr John Garside
Thirsk, North Yorkshire

Pole vaulting into a hotel bed

SIR – We have just returned from a night away and for the second time I discovered that, while our hotel bed was luxuriously comfortable, it was too high off the floor. The only way I succeeded in getting onto the bed was in a most undignified fashion with my husband pushing my posterior and catapulting me into the air so I landed spread-eagled like a stranded whale.

If hotels are determined to pursue this high-bed culture, I feel they should provide either a trampoline or a vaulting pole.

Margaret Hancock
Yateley, Hampshire

SIR – Why are hotel rooms so full of unnecessary cushions? On a recent visit to an Oxfordshire hotel I counted no fewer than seven piled up on the bed like a mini mountain range.

William Foot
Walberton, West Sussex

SIR – There should be a tight corner in hell reserved for the designers of duvet covers with very small openings.

As an American friend of mine once put it, it's like trying to push 2lbs of melted butter up a wildcat's rear end with a red-hot gimlet.

Graham Masterton
Tadworth, Surrey

Loose screw

SIR – I was highly amused by your recent article about handling the father-in-law from hell. Fortunately my husband seems to have a very good relationship with his future son-in-law, and when they recently moved into a new property, my husband went over to help with some DIY.

Struggling with a screw fitting, my husband asked if he had any lubricant. Future son-in-law (English not being his first language) disappeared into the bedroom and came back a few minutes later proffering a tube of KY jelly.

Husband politely declined and suggested olive oil instead.

Shirley Batten-Smith
Watford, Hertfordshire

All the Presidents Club men

SIR — My father used to say that when an Englishman drank too much he became mildly amorous and very boring. After the furore of the Presidents Club, it looks as if they will have to make do with the latter.

John Rawlins
Bishops Caundle, Dorset

SIR — At the risk of being vilified, I feel it should also be noted that drunken women in a similar scenario are not much better. I have witnessed alcohol-fuelled hen parties doing much the same to male waiters; on one particular occasion one poor chap was chased on to a table and denuded by a phalanx of baying women.

The remaining waiters locked themselves in the kitchen until the venue had been cleared.

(Ms) H. Gelder
Hillmorton, Warwickshire

SIR — And to cap it all, the apostrophe had been omitted from the club's name.

Bob Shute
Bradford-on-Avon, Wiltshire

#MaeToo

SIR — I wonder what Mae West, with her aphorism "Better to be looked over than to be overlooked", would have made of the #MeToo movement?

Alan Duncalf
Bampton, Devon

SIR — You can imagine my dismay many years ago when my wonderful 65-year-old secretary asked if she could have a private word with me, a young managing director, about sexual harassment.

After sitting down in my office she said: "Yes, I'm not getting enough of it."

Tim Williams
Hungerford, Berkshire

SIR — The only positive aspect to the ban on wolf whistling is that I can tell myself that its illegality is the reason I no longer attract such attention.

Jennie Gibbs
Goring-by-Sea, West Sussex

SIR — When I was in the Air Force, in the 1950s, one of the girls in our billet had a date with an airman at the camp cinema. An hour later she came storming back in. We asked her what had happened.

"He lobbed his thing into my hand so I stubbed my cigarette out on it. He won't do that again."

Changed days.

Jacqueline McCrindle
Prestwick, Ayrshire

SIR — When I left school to go to college in the late 1950s, my grandmother, who was born in 1876, advised me to carry a hatpin in my handbag. The pin was quite a common accessory at that time, judging by the number of yelps one heard when visiting the cinema.

Pam McEntyre
Mollington, Cheshire

SIR – When growing up, I was told that it was bad manners to walk around with one's hands in one's pockets. However, it would seem that this is now the safest option for us men.

James Richardson
Bexhill-on-Sea, East Sussex

SIR – I was somewhat nonplussed by the seemingly over-familiar presence of the lady immediately behind me in the bus queue on a recent visit to Majorca. It was only later that I realised her accomplice had removed my wallet from the side-pocket of my shorts.

Mike Leaper
Eastbourne, East Sussex

SIR – My wife, squeezing between tables at our bridge club, apologised when she brushed accidentally against an elderly, retired Perthshire farmer.
He replied: "It's a'richt, lassie. The spirit is willing, but the engine's buggered."

George K. McMillan
Perth

SIR – Hopefully the current furore regarding inappropriate sexual contact will signal an end to the awkward continental habit of intrusive social kissing and a welcome return to the safe British handshake.

Jan Bardey
Kineton, Warwickshire

Neutralising clothing choice

SIR — What a fuss about how to display children's clothes. Why not call the rails "clothes often chosen by boys" and "clothes often chosen by girls". That should keep everyone happy.

Matty Thacker
Tanworth-in-Arden, Warwickshire

SIR — Kilts are the answer for all.

Deirdre Lay
Cranleigh, Surrey

SIR — It is with great shock I read that Marks & Spencer is to shut 100 stores by 2022. Where is middle England to buy its underwear? Or can we expect the inhibited Brits to "go commando"?

Guy Bennett
Claygate, Surrey

SIR — I notice in a local Marks & Spencer that there were many styles of jeans labelled Straight, but none marked LGBT. A missed opportunity, perhaps?

Chris Burdon
Rushmere St Andrew, Suffolk

Sit down, shut up

SIR — A lengthy visit to the lavatories in a trendy modern cinema complex gave me time to reflect on the current debate on gender-neutral facilities. Along with a dozen or so fellow queue-ers of various genders, I waited for one of five cubicles to become available, there being no urinals at all in the building.

Surely the most sensible, efficient (and gender-neutral) method would be to have doors labelled "urinals" and "cubicles". Individuals able to conduct their business while standing would use the former; anyone wishing or needing to sit down, the latter.

> **Dr Martin Shutkever**
> Pontefract, West Yorkshire

SIR – I cannot understand the controversy over "gender-neutral lavatories" since they are to be found in every home in the country.

> **G. Johnson**
> Gateshead, Tyne and Wear

Good Dave Hunting

SIR – I am appalled at the news that there are fewer women CEOs than CEOs called Dave. This is clearly discriminatory against not only female executives but also all men who don't have the good fortune to be called Dave.

> **Keith Valentine**
> Tunbridge Wells, Kent

SIR – If women are able to do the same job as men for less salary it begs the question: why employ men at all?

> **Elizabeth Hall**
> Bradninch, Devon

SIR — Regarding the role of men and women, I believe that my dear Grandfather Joe may have been well ahead of the game.

On learning that his wife Annie was feeling unwell he magnanimously observed: "Well, if you are not feeling better by teatime, I'll give you a hand with the washing up."

David Belcher
Thatcham, Berkshire

Keep clean and carry on

SIR — Your article on circumcision reminded me of a story told by a girlfriend many years ago. Her fellow students at a convent school had discovered that a biblical passage referring to foreskins would be used in a forthcoming lesson.

Accordingly, a selected girl raised her hand and asked: "Please, Sister Francis, what are foreskins?"

Without batting an eyelid, the young nun replied, "Why, the skin from their forehead, of course" — and calmly carried on.

John Martin
Soberton, Hampshire

SIR — My four-year-old daughter asked me why boys stood up to pee. Deciding she was probably ready for some basic anatomy, I asked her what little boys had that little girls didn't have. She thought about it for a few seconds, and then said: "Action Man?"

Rita Coppillie
Liskeard, Cornwall

Suffer the little children

SIR – Some years ago, the church in south London where I sang removed some Victorian pews and moved them to the back of the church where they formed a "benched off" area for a creche. This became known as the King Herod Memorial Corner.

Hilary Bentley
Alderney, Guernsey

SIR – When our daughter was going through the "terrible twos", I asked our vicar if he could administer a "booster" baptism, as the first one hadn't taken. Sadly, he thought I was being serious.

Dr Peter West
Bosham, West Sussex

SIR – I have just received a guarantee for a new garage roof that excludes acts of God. I find this phrase somewhat anachronistic and I am sure that a more rigorous term could be devised.

After all, atheists would deny that there was any such thing, while fundamentalists would hold that even a light drizzle is an act of God.

Roger Jackson
Heaton Moor, Cheshire

SIR – Further to the letter regarding the "Knit & Natter" sessions introduced into her local library, our local church has had a similar group for several years now, universally known as "Stitch & Bitch".

Roger Brimble
South Croydon, Surrey

Here . . . comes . . . the . . . .

SIR – As a church organist I have often had to play for a long time while awaiting a bride. My record is 45 minutes. When I was in the Philippines, I knew of a priest who always began the wedding service on time, whether the bride was present or not.

Robert Ascott
Eastbourne, East Sussex

SIR – My husband and I exchanged rings 56 years ago. The vicar had no idea what to do: after my husband had endowed me with all his worldly goods I had to repeat the same promise, thus giving them all back to him. He reminds me from time to time.

Judy Kirk
Littleover, Derbyshire

Over her dead body

SIR – So many of my excellent suggestions and ideas are met with my wife's response: "Over my dead body".

When she dies, I am going to have her cremated. Her ashes will be put in a Royal Navy brass shell case from the Great War, which currently contains the poker and brush in the drawing-room hearth. This will be sealed and lowered into a recess that I will dig on the threshold of the back door.

Each time I leave the house it will be over her dead body. Everything will then be possible.

Peter J. Robinson
Lichfield, Staffordshire

The affronted room

SIR — Inspired by universities appointing safe-space marshals, I decided to declare the living room a safe space where my wife was no longer allowed to insult me. Having informed her of this new arrangement, she called me a cretinous buffoon.

Is there a safe-space regulatory body, or does this count as a hate crime I can refer to the police?

Paul Atkins
St Albans, Hertfordshire

Advertising your age

SIR — A measure of one's age used to be that policemen looked so young. That's not so easy now given that one seldom sees the police.

What I've noticed as I've got older is that the actors in Funeral Plan advertisements look like mere youngsters.

John Kirkham
Woodford Green, Essex

SIR — Getting old is when your grandchild looks at your wife's loyal kitchen gadget and says: "That is quite an antique; it could be worth a lot of money."

Jonathan E. Godrich
Clee St Margaret, Shropshire

SIR – Would you kindly stop telling those of us who live alone that we are lonely.

It is making us feel lonely.

Donald Mcnab
Whitchurch by Tavistock, Devon

SIR – Will Tracey Crouch, the new Minister For Loneliness, be given departmental staff, or will she have to face the job alone?

Phil Sharman
Herne Bay, Kent

SIR – On a Royal British Legion tour abroad it seemed to be agreed by women of a certain age that the biggest catch is not a man with good looks, nor with brains or even with money, but a man who had a car and was still driving.

Anthony Appleby
Exeter

SIR – I do so look forward to the day when I'm told that I look too young to travel on my Senior Railcard.

Juliet Bothams
Binsted, Hampshire

SIR – For years now I have been living in the diminishing hope that a shopkeeper would require some identification to prove my age when purchasing a bottle of wine.

That hope has now been finally extinguished when my barber asked whether I was entitled to the OAP discount.

Downhill from now on, then.

Julian Waters
Standford, Hampshire

SIR – I am currently 70 years old and am still managing occasionally to "trip up" coming out of the pub. At what age do I describe such an episode as "having had a fall"?

Anthony Peter Bolton
Stretton, Shropshire

Critical drinking

SIR – I can only concur with the research undertaken by Oxford University into the beneficial sound of a cork being drawn from a bottle of wine. On many occasions my wife and I have described this as "the happy thuck".

Andrew Reid
Campsea Ashe, Suffolk

SIR – My bottle of wine tonight stated: "Best enjoyed young and cold". But I am old and hot: what shall I do?

Bernard Wilson
Ramsbottom, Lancashire

SIR – I've just bought a box of wine from a major supermarket on which is the sticker: "Lasts for six weeks from opening".

I only wish that were possible.

Alan Green
Moreton-in-Marsh, Gloucestershire

SIR — I read that I need to reduce my alcohol intake. Having just retired I was looking forward to my regular 5pm tipple. May my wife transfer her 14 units to me, given that she is teetotal?

Paul Vince
Steeple Ashton, Wiltshire

SIR — If drinking six glasses of wine a week knocks two years off your life, I must already be dead.

Greig Bannerman
Frant, East Sussex

SIR — As Winston Churchill clearly knew, and lived long to prove it: alcohol is a preservative.

Diana Spencer
Herne Bay, Kent

SIR — I see you have stopped reviewing beer in the Saturday edition. Can it be because the ridiculous modern trend of massively overdoing the hop has exhausted your stock of phrases to describe something that tastes like it has come out of the wrong end of a cat?

Joe Kerrigan
London W13

SIR — I have it on the authority of my son, who was deployed to the South Atlantic guard ship as an RNR officer, that gin and tonic is not the same unless made with ice chipped from a glacier on South Georgia.

Charly Lowndes
Malvern, Worcestershire

SIR – I wonder how many people guffawed when it was reported that airport operators say they sell alcohol responsibly. Whenever I fly from Manchester, it's nearly always before breakfast, but even then it feels like I've been transported into one of the seamier Hogarth paintings.

Nick Gillibrand
Carnforth, Lancashire

SIR – I have always looked at knitting bags with the utmost suspicion since my grandmother declared that a cylindrical one was the ideal hiding place for a bottle of whisky. She made this discovery while staying in a hotel that had no licence.

Liz Young
Long Marston, Hertfordshire

SIR – What is this nonsense about Dry Januarys and now Sober Octobers? I abstain for half the year: I never touch a drop between midnight and midday.

Nicholas Diment
Emsworth, Hampshire

SIR – Shortly after Christmas my partner and I were told that, every time someone chose to have a "Dry January", somewhere in the world a barman died.

On that, we decided upon a Moist January with occasional damp patches.

Peter Sumner
Ruan Minor, Cornwall

The right sort of weather

SIR — Given the admission by Keith Richards in your interview that he has recently given up drink and drugs, perhaps the current downturn in the weather is in fact hell freezing over.

Tom Erskine
Castel, Guernsey

SIR — Even though the weather in February was atrocious our milkman still delivered the milk.

Perhaps the dairy should bid to run a rail franchise.

Steve Urwin
Great Linford, Buckinghamshire

SIR — Our milk was also delivered on time as usual. We did, however, have to put it in the fridge to thaw it out.

Allan Kirtley
Chobham, Surrey

SIR — I have found a use for the rubber bands discarded by Royal Mail.

A couple of bands slipped over the widest part of each shoe gives a little more grip when stepping out these frosty mornings to collect *The Daily Telegraph*.

Tony Greatorex
Syston, Leicestershire

SIR — While driving in a blizzard through Leeds city centre, I witnessed a traffic warden brushing the snow off the windscreen of an abandoned car and placing a parking ticket behind the wiper. I hope the recipient tore it up.

Sue McFarland
Little Bytham, Lincolnshire

SIR – Listening to Radio 4, I was pleased to hear a school mistress defending a pupil's right to throw snowballs against a school master who had banned the annual fun. Then she spoilt it all by saying she preferred to build a "snow person".

Heaven help us all.

David Mawson
Chesterfield, Derbyshire

SIR – Having donned my arctic gear in order to go to the supermarket I called at my elderly neighbour's house to ask if anything was required.

"200 cigarettes, a bag of toffees and next week's TV guide," came the reply.

Vera Shaw
Maidenhead, Berkshire

SIR – I visited my local supermarket this weekend for the first time since reports that the great British public has been panic buying for essentials in the bad weather.

Sure enough, many shelves had been picked bare. Bread? Fine. Chicken? Okay. Bottled water? Sensible. But strawberries? Is irony finally dead?

Nick Dillon
Hasketon, Suffolk

SIR — My husband's only concession to the present cold temperatures was to dig a path from the utility back door to the various dustbins, in order that I could get there more easily.

I very much appreciated his kindness.

Judith A. Scott
St Ives, Cambridgeshire

SIR — Could the Met Office issue me with a wind chill factor for my wife's hands and feet at bedtime?

Charles Pressley
Goring-by-Sea, West Sussex

SIR — The travelling difficulties associated with February's bad weather led many to heed the authorities' advice to work from home. This has led to a new word in our house: *gumfing* (getting under my feet).

Gabriella Gordon
Thames Ditton, Surrey

SIR — Now that the snow is thawing, will the drivers of 4 x 4s stop looking so smug and superior?

Peter Lally
Broseley, Shropshire

The annual grind

SIR — Spring must be on its way. The sun is streaming through an open window and faintly in the distance I can hear my first angle grinder.

Terry Warburton
Leighton Buzzard, Bedfordshire

SIR – In early March I go into the garden, catch hold of winter by the throat and ritually strangle it. The incantation I chant at the same time is unprintable but effective.

Roy Jones
Quorn, Leicestershire

SIR – After the last few summers that we've endured, isn't it a refreshing change to grumble about the heat?

Alan Thomas
Caerphilly, Glamorgan

SIR – In the drought of 1976, South West Water Authority suggested that its customers "shower with a friend". When will the Environment Agency ask us to "blush not flush"?

David Latham
Great Shelford, Cambridgeshire

SIR – This summer is no match yet for that of 1976. My wife and I were married on 28 August that year, after nearly three months with no rain. We had Handel's Water Music played at our wedding and, sure enough, it rained right on cue.

The vicar had ammunition for at least three sermons in the following weeks.

James Farrington
Colemans Hatch, East Sussex

SIR – In the summer of 1976 we recycled every drop we could, including using bath water to irrigate the vegetables.

We had a bumper crop of healthy, succulent cucumbers, but we couldn't eat any of them. They all tasted of Lifebuoy soap.

Liz Wicken
Foxton, Cambridgeshire

SIR — Following the last hose-pipe ban, my local pub posted a notice outside which read: "Owing to water shortages, beer will now be served only at full strength."

Sandy Pratt
Storrington, West Sussex

SIR — How many times must I refrain from running the tap while cleaning my teeth in order to save enough water to fill my neighbour's swimming pool?

Janet Williams
Chudleigh, Devon

The Cork weather scale

SIR — If the Met Office is thinking of adopting local dialects to describe degrees of rain, they could do worse than the slang we used when we lived in Cork.

1: *Soft* (Misty); 2: *Spitting* (Light spots); 3: *Squally* (Rainy and windy); 4: *Pissing* (A regular shower); 5: *Flogging* (Heavyish rain); 6: *Lashing* (Very heavy rain); 7: *Bull rain* (You wouldn't put a dog out in it); 8: *Bucketing* (Holy Mother of God); 9: *Pelting* (By the Lord Harry); 10: *Milling out of the Heavens* (It Must Be August).

Graham Masterton
Tadworth, Surrey

SIR – Here in South Lincolnshire we have had a lazy wind. It would rather go through you than round you.

Doug Braybrooks
Cowbit, Lincolnshire

SIR – I yearn for the return of those weather maps of yesteryear with their distinct isobars, warm fronts and the occasional "occluded thingy".

Ross Ellens
Stony Stratford, Buckinghamshire

Too much information

SIR – I store vast amount of data, including personal details, images and unverified information on other people, in a supercomputer called "brain".

While usually secure, it has been known to inadvertently share information when hacked via the "alcohol" malware.

I have not informed all of the people whose data I hold.

This data is intended to be stored on a lifetime basis.

All data will be destroyed at some unknown future date.

Please advise me how I would proceed under the General Data Protection Regulation.

Keith Farrow
Chippenham, Wiltshire

SIR – While giving a lift to my nephew the other day I asked him about his taste in music. He gave a shrug and said that he streamed his music from Spotify. He then revealed that, on International Women's Day, Spotify had messaged him to say that he wasn't listening to much music from female artists. Spotify had monitored his listening and sent him a score.

I look forward to my credit card telling me that I spend too much on alcohol, and my electricity supplier telling me that I am staying up too late for my health.

Gwilym Hughes
Littlehampton, West Sussex

SIR – Given the furore over the possible misuse of Facebook personal data, perhaps now is the time to give some publicity to the little known Hereford Quill Pen Society which aims to take us back 200 years.

For a modest fee members are issued with a quill pen, and a small club hammer with which to smash any piece of electronic equipment with which they come into contact.

Michael Hawthorne
Madley, Herefordshire

SIR – I have received a "permission to hold my data" GDPR email from a funeral company of which I have never heard, in which they told me that I was a "valued customer".

I am wondering who has been masquerading as me – or whether I have actually used their services and now exist in a reincarnated form.

There is hope yet for an afterlife.

Martin Watts
Chalfont St Giles, Buckinghamshire

SIR – Royal Mail is encouraging businesses to use unaddressed mail to get round new EU laws. I intend to stop putting junk mail in my recycling bin and instead use the bright red one at the end of the street which the Post Office has kindly provided.

Brian Donaldson
Orrell, Lancashire

SIR — My late father dealt with junk mail by endorsing each item with a clip-art style image of two fingers making the V sign, above a seven-letter caption which both started and finished with the letter F.

Then he posted it back.

B.R.
Billericay, Essex

SIR — Among the many emails sent to me about the GDPR, one of the more confusing is from an IT company which advises me: "If in doubt contact us immodestly."

Philip Wright
London SW11

Dumb technology

SIR — Having just purchased my first smartphone at the age of 76, I now understand why everyone is walking around staring at their phones.

They are trying to understand them.

Ralph Barnes
Christchurch, Dorset

SIR — I see that WhatsApp is down. I wonder how many people will suddenly find out that their handheld devices can also make phone calls.

Robin Whiting
Castle Rising, Norfolk

SIR — I need to be very careful in the kitchen when using my iPad Pro tablet.

It's identical in size to our kitchen scales.

Stephen Gledhill
Chadbury, Worcestershire

SIR — With all the advanced technology in this world, how is it that, as usual, I have cut my thumb when opening a tin of corned beef?

Susan Apedaile
Sheffield

SIR — With the demise of the Yellow Pages, how will strong men or women demonstrate their strength now?

Thomas Wood
Lastingham, North Yorkshire

SIR — My smart meter is so secure that even my electricity supplier cannot get information out of it.

S. McVey
Kingsdown, Kent

SIR — Front-page headline of *The Daily Telegraph*: "'Smart homes' will tell you to get off the sofa".

I don't need a "smart home" to tell me that — I already have a wife.

John Fox
Stamford, Lincolnshire

SIR — It is often observed that pets and their owners become alike over the years. Could the same be said for computers? Ours is dictatorial and slow.

Carole King
Ilfracombe, Devon

SIR — In light of my husband's craving for North Korea's superior broadband service, I have unselfishly suggested he relocate.

Diane Learmont-Hughes
Caldy, Wirral

SIR — One of my son's early habits was to call all phones "Daddy". I may have been working too hard at the time.

M.S.
London E1

SIR — My wife received an Amazon Echo for Christmas and we have found it to be interesting and enjoyable to use.

We have noticed lately, however, that Alexa has started to interject in conversations with her own advice and, whether or not she is becoming hard of hearing or plainly disobedient, she is refusing commands to "stop".

Should I be worried that this is the beginning of a robot takeover?

Stephen Ennis
Thames Ditton, Surrey

SIR — When robots go on strike, will humans do their work?

David Rumsey
Pinner, Middlesex

Silly seasonal salutations

SIR — As I tackle the annual task of writing my Christmas cards to relatives and friends, I like to add random salutations on the envelopes: Sir, Lady, MBA, OBE, Brexiteer etc.

I feel it brings a little Christmas cheer to those who carry the cards on their journey and to those who finally receive them.

P.C.-M.
Gustard Wood, Hertfordshire

SIR — Our daughter's Christmas card reached us on 9 January from London, having been posted and postmarked on 12 December. By my calculation that exactly matches the speed of a sloth, at 0.15mph.

I wonder if Royal Mail could save money by using these very attractive animals to carry our post without any loss of efficiency.

Mike Owen
Claverdon, Warwickshire

SIR — I have profound sympathy for the poor dolphins, sharks, tuna etc. that become entangled in abandoned filament netting, having required urgent help to unravel myself from similar material encasing our recently delivered Christmas tree.

J.A. Morgan
Churchill, Oxfordshire

SIR – For me the first manifestation of the miracle of Christmas is when last year's lights instantly work.

R.A. Collings
Presteigne, Powys

SIR – You quote a Wiccan student objecting to a proposed Solstice Event at Cambridge, as it is "using a holiday I celebrate with religious conviction as merely the theme for a party".

I know how she feels – every Christmas.

Shirley Puckett
Tenterden, Kent

SIR – I am looking forward to a peaceful Christmas alone again this year. There is only one problem: how do you pull a Christmas cracker on your own without cheating?

Marie Jones
Wallington, Surrey

SIR – I suggest that the drone shooting season should start a few days after Christmas. They could be taken down, like the decorations, on ("The Glorious") Twelfth Night.

Tim Garland
Bathford, Somerset

SIR – One Christmas I decided to impress my congregation by hiring a donkey for the children's Crib Service. After the ceremony the donkey was led to the church doorway for our final hymn. I thanked everyone for attending, then thanked the donkey, which brayed loudly before emptying its bowels.

It took some time before we could clear the contents
away in order to release the congregation.

> **Canon Alan Hughes**
> Berwick-upon-Tweed, Northumberland

SIR – A £175 bill for taking my Springer Spaniel to the vets
at 1am on Boxing Day. It had consumed an entire Yule Log.

> **Michael Cattell**
> Mollington, Cheshire

SIR – Five years ago, my son (then single) gave his sister's
first child a drum for her first Christmas. He followed this
up with a xylophone the following year. I knew my daughter
had not forgiven him.

This year my daughter gave my son's first daughter an
accordion for her first Christmas.

I am watching this escalating musical arms race with
much enjoyment and will only intervene when the
neighbours start complaining.

> **John O'Neill**
> Hessle, East Yorkshire

SIR – After the surfeit of leaflets encouraging the purchase
of festive food, Christmas seems officially over when the
slimming leaflets start dropping through the door.

> **Linda Bos**
> Midhurst, West Sussex

Better before

SIR – "Co-op sells out-of-date food for just 10p", says
your headline.

This isn't news.

Our local Co-op has been selling out-of-date food for years, unintentionally and at full price.

Moira H.R. Brodie
Bourton, Wiltshire

SIR — The younger generation in my family hold up their hands in horror whenever they find items in my kitchen past their sell-by dates. They have yet to discover that last week they consumed a dish containing a tin of tomatoes with a sell-by date of 2002.

To my knowledge, they have all survived.

Sue Johns
Clifton-upon-Teme, Worcestershire

SIR — If our children are brought up on grapes without pips, how will they learn to spit?

Ian Smethurst
Congleton, Cheshire

SIR — The recent cold snap has provided the opportunity to investigate the darkest depths of the freezer. I found a haggis dated best before January 2008. Sadly I was forbidden to eat it but the dogs enjoyed it.

The blackbirds also enjoyed an unopened 20-year-old packet of shredded wheat.

Ian McMullen
Doddington, Kent

SIR — I wonder how your more germ-obsessive readers would have reacted to my experience a few weeks ago. I had just spread whipped cream over a chocolate roulade on the kitchen worktop prior to rolling it up when Agatha, my Siamese, came bounding in through the cat flap.

Finding her route to the kitchen sink, where she takes all her prey, impeded by the roulade, she dropped her mouse right in the middle of the cream.

I picked up the poor creature, still alive but smothered in cream, and transported it back out through the cat flap. I smoothed over the disturbed cream and completed the roulade, which was devoured at a family gathering amid much laughter after I had related the story.

My sister remarked that she hoped Agatha didn't now expect all her mice to have cream on.

Beryl Salisbury
Llanfairynneubwll, Anglesey

The raising of Hammy

SIR – As young boys my two sons had hamsters as pets and one morning we found one of them apparently dead in the bottom of its cage.

Trying to soften the blow for the children, I went to great lengths to explain that Hammy had gone to baby Jesus and would have lots of hamster friends in heaven. Together we made a coffin for the hamster and his toys. We chose and prepared a burial site in the garden but, as I carefully lifted the "body" out of its cage to place into the shoebox coffin, Hammy underwent what can only be described as a Lazarus moment, terrifying us out of our skins.

I wished I'd known sooner about hibernating hamsters.

Jennie Allen
Baildon, West Yorkshire

The hardest woof

SIR — At a National Trust property I saw a sign stating: "Sorry, no dogs".

There was no need to apologise; I wasn't expecting any.

John Curran
Bristol

SIR — Thank you so much for your very helpful article listing the UK's 25 most dog-friendly pubs.

I shall keep it for reference of places to avoid at all costs.

Robin Lane
Devizes, Wiltshire

SIR — In the pet foods aisle of a local Aldi I recently encountered a middle-class couple pushing a trolley full of food and alcohol. As they contemplated a display of dog treats the man said to his wife: "We can't buy his food from here."

John Birch
Waterfoot, Lancashire

SIR — I have a bag full of different bags for life but am unsure of the correct protocols for their use. For example, my wife will not take an Aldi bag into Waitrose but will produce a Waitrose bag in Aldi.

A Sainsbury's checkout lady regarded me with obvious disapproval when I used an Aldi bag but seemed to accept a Tesco bag without demur.

Peter Heap
Manuden, Hertfordshire

The low path

SIR — How bizarre for GPs to suggest people combat depression by taking a stroll alongside their local canal.

One suspects that half an hour of staring at dead dogs, discarded tyres, dumped supermarket trolleys and other floating detritus could well be the final straw and result in many of the poor souls jumping in.

> **Charles Garth**
> Ampthill, Bedfordshire

SIR — Further to the revelations about the Irwell being the most polluted river in the world, I recall that in the 1950s it was one of the few places where one could play "Pooh-sticks" with real poo. Simple pleasures in those days.

> **Martin Mayer**
> Chorley, Lancashire

A close brush

SIR — Lavatory brushes are dreadful things. My wife bought one, which I used once before reverting to paper.

> **Frank Wilkinson**
> Lostock, Lancashire

SIR — Can I add my support to the campaign for real plates? I was once unfortunate enough to have my meal served on a ceramic tile which was of a design I have only ever seen in public lavatories.

> **Toby St Leger**
> Oldmeldrum, Aberdeenshire

Strawing berries

SIR – Before plastic straws are banned make sure you have a supply for a brilliant way to hull strawberries. Push the straw straight up from the pointed end of the strawberry and the core and greenery will come away cleanly.

Joan Guest
Epping, Essex

SIR – I cut up plastic straws to draw lots for our regular Monday tennis four. My partner always seems to draw the short straw. Would she have better luck with paper straws?

G. Marling-Roberts
Sowley, Hampshire

SIR – Keep some straws in the DIY box for blowing debris out of drill holes without getting it back in your eye. Use the rest for table-top blow football and showing disbelieving children how you managed to hit the back of a teacher's neck with a dried pea every time (wife at kitchen sink is a good substitute, albeit politically incorrect).

Victor Launert
Matlock Bath, Derbyshire

SIR – Now that the order has gone out to ban plastic "stirrers", I finally understand what those irritating and dangerous bits of plastic are for.

I had assumed that they were to slow consumption: after a few large gin and tonics they either went up your nose or in your eye and you couldn't get at the drink at all.

Andrew Perrins
Upton-upon-Severn, Worcestershire

SIR – Flower arrangers often resort to a discarded twig in the absence of a teaspoon.

> **Suzie Carter**
> Woodcote Green, Worcestershire

SIR – When calculators superseded slide rules in the 1970s, we research engineers were not universally impressed. You could not stir your tea with a calculator.

> **David Marsh**
> Countesthorpe, Leicestershire

SIR – Many moons ago I watched a colleague use the blunt end of a cheap Biro to stir his tea.

It seemed to work well, but the interesting trickle of blue ink seemed to put him quite off the tea.

> **P. Gascoyne**
> Wantage, Oxfordshire

SIR – A Biro top is most efficient for cleaning ears.

> **Simon McIlroy**
> Croydon, Surrey

SIR – I have a solution to the environmental damage caused by disposable coffee cups which was very effective in the past: have a cup of coffee at home before you go out.

> **Angus Cameron**
> Ball Hill, Berkshire

SIR – With all the talk about banning single-use plastics, how about adding the new plastic £5 and £10 notes to the list? I only use them once before they disappear from my wallet.

Dag Pike
Bristol

SIR – We had a plumber in last week. When he asked for an old towel to mop up, I gave him a nappy. The child who last used it is now 48. How's that for recycling?

Patricia Lister
Poulton-le-Fylde, Lancashire

Vaping wind-up

SIR – My wife and I were recently assaulted by a huge cloud of noxious vapour in our local park. The gentleman, in reply to my complaint, said: "Vaping is not smoking therefore it is legal."

I then farted upwind of him.

His face was a picture when I said farting was not smoking.

Ian Stirton Smith
Gosport, Hampshire

Slim pickings

SIR – One of my wife's friends joined a running club then proceeded to run off with one of the members. As a result my wife wouldn't allow me to join a running club. I mentioned joining a slimming club and asked if she would mind as I might be tempted to run off with a fat lass. She didn't.

I trudged off to my first Slimming World meeting last night.

Garry Gibson
Jedburgh, Roxburghshire

SIR – Today I took delivery of a new set of bathroom scales that were manufactured in China. One of the instructions reads: "Do not put objects rudely onto this scale".

I'm wondering whether I ought to put some clothes on before weighing myself.

Ronnie Cleave
Winkleigh, Devon

SIR – You recommend a lie-in as the key to staying in shape.

I remained in bed for an extra 90 minutes this morning, eating my fresh fruit and yogurt and reading the *Telegraph*. I then weighed myself to find I had not lost weight – please advise.

Jane Kaminski
Downham Market, Norfolk

SIR – First we hear that coffee is good for us, then that extra sleep is good for us.

Now all we need is for a professional body to tell us that chocolate is good for us, and life will be perfect.

Margaret Hart
Romsey, Hampshire

SIR – I very much doubt that the proposal by the Royal College of Paediatrics and Child Health to ban fast food outlets within 400 yards of every school in the country would have any impact on pupils' diets.

At the very least, however, it may provide them with some exercise.

Adam Tindall
Dollar, Clackmannanshire

SIR – First fat, now sugar. Whatever happened to the land of milk and honey?

Richard Osborne
Eton, Berkshire

SIR – Overheard at a birthday party.
"Wouldn't your friend like some cake?"
"No, thanks, she doesn't eat cake."
"Why doesn't she like cake?"
"She can't have any because she's diabolical."

Graham Watson
Yeovil, Somerset

SIR – There is a perfectly good, inexpensive diet: boiled cabbage and gravy. It works every time on Labradors.

Charles Trollope
Colchester, Essex

SIR – I bought some kale in Princetown, Devon, last year. Having found it somewhat challenging for myself, I offered the remainder to the first Dartmoor pony I met.

He sniffed it, looked me in the eye, turned on his heel and walked off.

Bill Boutcher-West
Grateley, Hampshire

SIR — It is most irritating, on return from a good walk, to find the business part of one's activity tracker at home on charge, and that one has been wearing the empty wristband. The dilemma — to go round again, or not?

Evelyn Weston
Bromley Cross, Lancashire

SIR — My NHS device recorded 200 more steps for a seven-hour motorway drive than it did for a seven-hour trek the following day, over the Carnedds, in North Wales. Beware NHS statistics.

Jacqueline King
Castle Cary, Somerset

Bare elbow syndrome

SIR — That "white coat syndrome" exists is indisputable. However, given that doctors are no longer allowed to wear said item, nor indeed suit and tie, perhaps it is time to re-name it?

I would suggest "bare elbow syndrome".

Dr Andrew Stoddart
Bexhill-on-Sea, East Sussex

SIR — Recent coverage of the risk of prostate cancer suggests digital rectal examination as a diagnostic. Digital? From experience, I can think of nothing less analogue.

Alex McIntosh
London SE3

SIR – Since I was widowed five years ago, the only
individual sharing my bed has been my lurcher. Should my
answer to the NHS's question about sexual orientation be:
"bestiality"?

> **Philip Barry**
> Lydden, Kent

SIR – The administration at the hospital where I was
formerly employed affixed a suggestion box on a wall in the
out-patients department. At the end of the first day it held
a single suggestion: "Please could you place the box a little
lower."

> **Godfrey Brangham**
> Usk, Monmouthshire

SIR – Many years ago my mother-in-law, on being
admitted to hospital, filled in the admittance form and
wrote "none" under religion.

Big mistake: all the faiths visited her in the hopes of a
conversion.

> **Yvonne Chappell**
> Ashtead, Surrey

SIR – On a visit to hospital last year I was asked by a doctor
if I was pregnant. This surprised me as I am a male of
mature years (with no transgender aspirations), albeit a
little portly.

> **Norman Macfarlane**
> Kingston upon Thames, Surrey

SIR – I was a teacher for many years. When in hospital after an operation the nurses tried to wake me up using my first name. I did not respond.

Someone on the other side of the ward said, "She's a teacher," so the nurse said, "'ere, Miss."

I shot up, wide awake and answered, "Yes?"

Brita Lakeman
Glentham, Lincolnshire

SIR – Might I advise the Royal College of Obstetricians and Gynaecologists that the average woman in labour frankly couldn't give a monkey's whether she is called by her first name, "she", "good girl" or the Queen of Sheba as long as they will just GET THAT BABY OUT RIGHT NOW.

Rachel Collins
Otterbourne, Hampshire

SIR – A surgeon has been fined for burning his initials on a patient's liver. Should I ever require liver surgery and there was someone with the necessary competence willing to undertake it, I would be happy for them to inscribe their entire curriculum vitae on said organ.

David Bell
Knowl Hill, Berkshire

SIR – Many years ago, a gillie on the river Spey, when responding to an urgent summons from a visiting angler to help him land a salmon, arrived just in time to see the guest, an orthopaedic surgeon, expertly kill the fish with a single blow from an unusual-looking "priest".

This turned out to be a titanium hip joint – recovered presumably from one of his less successful operations.

Andrew Yool
Pluscarden, Morayshire

SIR – If the NHS wants to learn how to speed up recovery times from major surgery, I suggest they immediately contact the production team of *Coronation Street*. Within two days of one character donating a kidney, and another character receiving said kidney, both are practically back to normal, and almost ready to leave hospital.

John Ball
Shoebury, Essex

SIR – One wonders how quickly the NHS problems would be resolved if our Ministers were to be struck down with the flu virus at a time when their private health providers went into liquidation.

M.J. Collins
Cowbeech, East Sussex

WESTMINSTER'S VILLAGE IDIOTS

A plague on both your Houses

SIR – I would like it known that I wish my ashes to be scattered through the air handling unit of the House of Commons. I will then at last get up the noses of all those who get up mine every time I pick up a newspaper.

Jay Roseveare
Yeovil, Somerset

SIR – In the 1920s an Italian flew over the parliament building in Rome, up-ending a chamber pot over it.

May we please ask some airman to perform the same function on behalf of the British public over Westminster?

Philip Wilson-Sharp
Canterbury

SIR – Theresa May is to draw up a code of conduct for MPs. This could be summed up in one sentence: "Don't do anything you wouldn't want to see on the front page of *The Daily Telegraph* tomorrow."

David L. Oliver
Langley, Berkshire

Honours in defeat

SIR – A knighthood is for a man who shows skill in battle, who is competent in equestrian jousting, and who, when finding himself at the foot of a castle with a fair maiden above him letting down her hair for him to climb, can reach her window.

I think Nick Clegg can do none of those things. I oppose his knighthood.

Philip Hodson
Newmarket, Suffolk

SIR – In March 1811 the septuagenarian John Purcell of County Cork was attacked in his home at night by nine burglars armed with a sawn-off shotgun. With his only weapon, a small folding knife, he killed two and severely wounded three before the remaining gang members fled.

Purcell was subsequently knighted by King George.

Nicholas Guitard
Poundstock, Cornwall

SIR – Could someone please explain what services to music Ringo Starr has provided?

Geoff Riley
Saffron Walden, Essex

SIR – One does not have to agree with him to acknowledge that Nigel Farage has made a significant contribution to the national debate in recent years – but obviously not as important as the observation that "we all live in a yellow submarine".

Julian Tope
Bristol

Dead Ukip wood

SIR – Both Henry Bolton and Donald Trump have promised to "Drain the Swamp".

Swamps support mangroves and other trees and a variety of interesting creatures. If they were to be drained, all one would be left with is a boring stretch of cracked dry mud and a lot of dead wood.

Peter Owen
Woolpit, Suffolk

SIR – Why does Ukip have a lion as their logo, when, as lions are not native to the UK, it is clearly an immigrant?

Sam Sayer
Rhyl, Denbighshire

SIR – I suggest that Ukip should urgently consider a merger with the Monster Raving Loony Party. This might well enhance the electability of both.

Anthony Bradbury
Newhaven, East Sussex

SIR – How many ex-leaders of Ukip can fit in a telephone box?

Ivor Davies
Chatham, Kent

SIR – Maybe, just maybe, Nigel Farage should learn how to disappear from the limelight with good grace.

Mark Boyle
Johnstone, Renfrewshire

Comrade Cob

SIR – Following the allegation by the former Czech spy Ján Sarkocy that Mr Corbyn was codenamed COB, I've found myself idly wondering who might have been CORN and what their relationship was to COB.

Martin Bastone
East Grinstead, West Sussex

SIR – Was Jeremy Corbyn merely trying to cache a small Czech?

Bill Wombell
Sheffield

SIR – I always enjoy Michael Deacon's Saturday musings. However, this week he described John McDonnell as "the future Chancellor". Please could you ask him to be more considerate: some of us are of a delicate nature politically and it takes us a while to recover from nightmares.

Mike Kaye
Norton, Lincolnshire

SIR – I for one would be pleased to see the Labour Party as "the government in waiting" in 2018 – and 2019, 2020, etc.

Ron Freedman
Toronto, Canada

SIR – Please tell me that Eddie Izzard joining Labour's NEC was your April Fool's joke.

Roy Hughes
Marlbrook, Worcestershire

SIR – Over the murder of a former Russian agent and his daughter on British soil Jeremy Corbyn will be "assertive, demanding and robust". Apart from using two- and even three-syllable words, what would he actually do?

Perhaps he plans to bore the Russians to death. Listening to him myself, I was almost on my knees pleading for mercy.

Dr Marius C. Felderhof
Birmingham

SIR – A court of law requires proof "beyond reasonable doubt".

Mr Corbyn requires "incontrovertible evidence".

Would a signed confession from Mr Putin be enough?

Janet Reed
Mirfield, West Yorkshire

SIR – Perhaps Jeremy Corbyn ought to consider going to live in Russia. He may look happier and smile a bit more.

Rosemary Corbin
Zeals, Wiltshire

SIR – I could almost understand Corbyn's knee-jerk support for Russia if it was still run by his nominally socialist comrades (itself a self-serving elite) – but the present regime is a kleptocracy with no socialist pretensions at all.

Perhaps Corbyn is still so rooted in the 1960s and 1970s that he is not yet aware of the events of 1989 and what followed.

Alan Beevor
Madron, Cornwall

SIR – It is highly unfair to decry Jeremy Corbyn's love of country. It is just that the country in question happens to be Venezuela.

Mark Hudson
Smarden, Kent

SIR – A couple of days before the last general election my wife and I realised a long-held dream by moving onto our new luxury barge. We joked that if Labour got into power we could always move our home to another country.

We have just enrolled at evening classes to brush up our French.

David Fouracre
Napton, Warwickshire

SIR – Jeremy Corbyn can simply go on holiday and come back when the Tory Party has self-destructed.

Coin Bridger
Frimley, Surrey

The roaming Right

SIR – Is Michael Gove's plan to open up the countryside in any way inspired by Mrs May's urge to run in fields of wheat?

Patrick van IJzendoorn
London SE3

SIR — Am I alone in thinking that Michael Gove ought to consider changing his spectacles for a pair that don't make him look like an owl?

Christine Lamagni
Swanage, Dorset

Mayday!

SIR — We have recently had the First of May: I am rather hoping to see the last of May.

Philip J. Honey
Retford, Nottinghamshire

SIR — Theresa May — just about managing.

Alan Lyall
Weston-super-Mare, Somerset

SIR — A friend recently received a letter addressed to the Prime Minister at 10 Downing Street, London. My friend lives at Number 10 in a street that begins with the letter D but is in Honiton in Devon.

We opened the letter (I know, but the temptation was too great), read it and then sealed it and sent it on its way. A week later another letter, also addressed to the PM in London, arrived at the Honiton address. Once again we had a quick read before sending it on its way. Now a third letter has been received.

It's all very mysterious, but most of all we feel sorry for the PM as she really does receive some bonkers letters.

Zanzie Griffin
Sheldon, Devon

SIR – Theresa May could quite happily ignore the gaggle of third-rate journalists, who now seem to spend most of their time shouting questions across Downing Street, if she had a pair of the latest bluetooth headphones and her favourite music on before she left the door of Number 10.

Lawrence Palmer
Edinburgh

SIR – There is speculation as to whether there will be a new leader of the Conservative Party, and, presumably, a new Prime Minister. I suggest that a novel way to evaluate the suitability of any candidate would be to examine their ability to write or recite limericks.

One of the best verses written by a Prime Minister is surely that contained in a letter Attlee wrote to his brother. Since it is well known I will quote another verse written by him in 1945:

> *They say I write limericks patly.*
> *That rumour I don't deny flatly.*
> *But this time I'm blowed*
> *If I don't write an ode*
> *On our victory, signed Clement Attlee.*

Of the current potential candidates we know that Mr Johnson won a prize for his rude limerick about the President of Turkey. I think that we should be told what abilities such people as Mr Hammond and Mr Rees-Mogg have in composing and reciting the old verse form.

In the interests of fairness, we should also invite responses from Jeremy Corbyn and Sir Vince Cable.

Dr Bob Turvey
Bristol

Mogg's stock

SIR – Having predicted Jeremy Corbyn's appearance at the Glastonbury Festival last year, I am pretty confident of seeing Jacob Rees-Mogg gracing the stage in 2018.

Whether or not his kaftan will be double-breasted remains to be seen.

Bob Stebbings
Chorleywood, Hertfordshire

Defenceless Secretary

SIR – In the case of Home Secretary Amber Rudd, the phrase having "the Prime Minister's full confidence" appears to mean holding up a corpse to shield her from incoming bullets.

Robert Langford
Keresley, Warwickshire

SIR – In the light of recent events, perhaps our next Prime Minister should appoint a Secretary of State for Consequences.

Stephen T.L. Phillips
Lanivet, Cornwall

SIR – Could someone please explain to me what on earth is wrong with setting targets for the removal of illegal immigrants? Indeed, should the target not be 100 per cent?

Captain Graham Sullivan RN (retd)
Gislingham, Suffolk

Cryptic currency

SIR – You report that 43 per cent of British adults aged 18 to 24 are confident that they understand Bitcoin. Doesn't this confirm that the rational part of the human brain isn't fully developed until the age of 25?

Nick Cowley
Nuthurst, West Sussex

SIR – Labour is campaigning for votes for 16-year-olds. In response, we should propose that all those over 50 years of age should have two votes. This will reflect our life experience, knowledge, our proven commitment to national life and our wisdom.

Peter Richards
Poole, Dorset

SIR – I remember the very first Bitcoin. It was the sixpence wrapped in foil inside my mother's homemade Christmas pudding.

Rob Marshall
Worcester

SIR – Due to the current economic uncertainty I am seriously thinking of keeping my Bitcoins under the mattress.

E.M. Haynes
Abingdon, Oxfordshire

Post-prime

SIR — The Deputy Governor of the Bank of England's use of the word "menopausal" to describe the state of the economy rebounded on him. What was more worrying was to see Ben Broadbent trying to reassure us that the economy is in fine shape while wearing charity shop shoes.

Alan Hughes
Berwick-upon-Tweed, Northumberland

SIR — Austerity must really be biting. It seems that every time we see a Minister marching towards Number 10 they are clutching a non-recyclable cup of coffee from Costa or Starbucks. Can Downing Street really not afford to make them a cup of coffee?

Geoffrey Nobes
Locks Heath, Hampshire

SIR — Some things seem better than they've been for years (unemployment, real wages, the FTSE); others are looking the worse for wear (retailing, sterling, the housing divide).
  As a 50-something female economics graduate, I'd say that "menopausal" about sums it up.

Ruth Corderoy
East Hagbourne, Oxfordshire

SIR — Perhaps Ben Broadbent could have saved himself an awful lot of opprobrium had he simply described the unproductive economy as "flaccid".

Sylvia More
Frodsham, Cheshire

Swinging Richard

SIR – It is believed that Big Ben was named after Sir Benjamin Hall, First Commissioner for Works at the Houses of Parliament, whose name is inscribed on the bell.

It is just as well his name was not Sir Richard Hall.

Tony Weller
Yate, Gloucestershire

Meet, greet, defeat

SIR – The slogan of the 1960s was: "Join the army, see the world, and meet people" – although there were derivatives, some of them pejorative.

Today, one might say, in the spirit of the MoD's new campaign, "Join the army, see the world, hug people, and each other."

Greg Waggett
Clare, Suffolk

SIR – Is the old song "Kiss Me Goodnight, Sergeant Major" about to become a reality?

Barbara Dixon
Mansfield, Nottinghamshire

SIR – When I was at Mons in 1965 we were addressed at our first parade ending with the words: "Remember, you are officer cadets so I call you Sir. I am the Regimental Sergeant Major so you call me Sir. The difference is that you mean it and I don't."

Simon Davey
Wilsford, Lincolnshire

SIR – I have no problem with women integrated into male units in barracks, just as in civilian offices, but women living alongside men is asking for trouble.

The Peshmerga in Iraq have the right idea with women-only combat units: these would certainly scare the hell out of me.

Lt Col Nick Moulton-Thomas
Oman

The metal of mettle

SIR – Regarding the debate about whether to put a statue of the late Baroness Thatcher in Parliament Square, apparently a statue of her has already been made out of bronze. Which humourless artist passed over the opportunity to immortalise the Iron Lady in the metal of her epithet?

Dewi Eburne
Cambridge

SIR – I saw the recently erected statue of Millicent Fawcett in Parliament Square. Not a bad effort technically, but why is she, a feminist icon, depicted waving a dishcloth apparently advertising beer ["Courage calls to courage everywhere"]?

They might as well have put her behind an ironing board.

Mark Stephens
Hungerford, Berkshire

Spot on, Minister

SIR — Too many universities generate increasing numbers of degrees which inevitably diminish their value.

Sir Humphrey Appleby in *Yes, Minister* had it right with his throw-away line: "We have to look after our universities — both of them."

Arthur W. J. G. Ord-Hume
Guildford, Surrey

Bercow's amateur dramatics

SIR — I am currently sitting outside a drama rehearsal room while my daughter practises a monologue about a monkey. I am passing the time reading the *Telegraph* online. At the precise moment that I opened today's story about John Bercow I heard my daughter screech: "That horrid little creature".

Coincidence?

David Jordan
Broad Town, Wiltshire

SIR — Is there any chance that tradition could be reversed, and MPs be allowed to drag the protesting Speaker away from the House of Commons Chair?

Tony Lank
Hurstpierpoint, West Sussex

SIR — Having survived yet again, is Mr Bercow in competition with Larry the Downing Street cat for who has the most lives?

Bill Hodgman
Gosport, Hampshire

Party animals

SIR — It is hardly surprising, given his weedy appellation, that Larry "The Lamb" is an ineffectual mouser. They should rename him Cromwell.

Richard George
St Albans, Hertfordshire

SIR — How refreshing to see that the Foreign Office cat, Palmerston, has been fulfilling his state duties conscientiously. My own solidly built ginger tom has also enjoyed the parliamentary summer recess, bringing home numerous mice and voles to my dispatch box.

His name? Boris.

Mike Hames
Cradley, Herefordshire

Bridge over troubled water

SIR — Building a bridge over the Channel, as Boris Johnson has suggested, does not strike me as an obvious way to "take back control of our borders".

Tim Beechey-Newman
Caversham, Berkshire

SIR – I fully support a bridge to France, but could we have one first?

George Bristow
Brading, Isle of Wight

SIR – I do applaud Boris Johnson's bridge-building ambitions across the Channel and to Northern Ireland. A trial run for those aspirations might be found, however, within his own party.

Andrew Johnston
Dumfries, Dumfriesshire

SIR – As one who walks on water, why does Boris need a bridge?

Dr P.E. Pears
Coleshill, Warwickshire

SIR – What happens when traffic from the UK, driving on the left, meets traffic from France driving on the right?

Peter Sauntson
Collyweston, Northamptonshire

SIR – Our Foreign Secretary, Boris Johnson, seems somewhat obsessed with nominal alliteration, whether it's bikes, buses, bridges or Brexit.

One feels that British influence abroad may be greater enhanced by a wider exploration of what the rest of the alphabet has to offer.

Graham Hoyle
Baildon, West Yorkshire

SIR –

Boris Johnson's Bridge of Size,
He eats far too many pies
To be allowed upon it.
(This is not a sonnet.)

Peter Wyton
Gloucester

SIR – An acrostic for Boris:
Bombastic
Outrageous
Ridiculous
Injudicious
Scruffy

Moira Merryweather
Worthen, Shropshire

SIR – Please could you ask Jo Johnson to take his brother along with him the next time he visits his barber and insist that Boris has the same style.

Lynne Waldron
Woolavington, Somerset

SIR – Is it cynical to suggest that Boris's threat to lie down before the bulldozers at Heathrow, if carried through, might ease two of Mrs May's problems in one fell stroke?

Colin Stone
St Cellardyke, Fife

SIR — Now that Boris Johnson no longer has a ministerial car it means he is on his bike. Thank heavens for that.

Terry Reeves
Coventry, Warwickshire

George of all trades

SIR — George Osborne has yet another job. Who does he think he is? Tony Blair?

C. Williams
Coedpoeth

Encore, Tony!

SIR — The more Tony Blair says that the voters got it wrong, the more determined people will be in favour of leaving the EU. More please, Mr Blair.

Anji Patterson
Camberley, Surrey

SIR — Tony Blair has said he is on the verge of setting up a new political party.

It will require a name. I suggest Brass Neck.

Graham Hitchcock
Bexleyheath, Kent

SIR — Tony Blair says Brexit would be an historic mistake. It takes one to recognise one.

Roger Welby-Everard
Caythorpe, Lincolnshire

Direct democracy

SIR – In view of his disdainful reference to "the tyranny of the majority", perhaps Kenneth Clarke might care to consider how he was elected to parliament.

Robin Denny
Windsor, Berkshire

Paying for the End of the Affair

SIR – The President of the EU parliament, Antonio Tajani, has described Britain's Brexit divorce bill offer of £20 billion as "peanuts".

The contribution represents around £500 per UK family. That's a heck of a lot of peanuts.

Eddie Hooper
Gravesend, Kent

SIR – If Brexit is a divorce then we are the party who should be claiming alimony, citing unreasonable behaviour by the other party.

Keith Horsfall
Swaffham, Norfolk

SIR – If I share a round of beers with 27 of my friends, I pay my share. But if I leave the pub before my friends, I do not keep paying their rounds for the next five years.

Jeremy Maddocks
London SW6

SIR — Will I be required to continue to pay towards the pension of the newest greenkeeper if I decide to leave the golf club?

Ian Goddard
Wickham, Hampshire

SIR — When considering the EU I am reminded of a comment by one of my schoolmasters to my class.

"Boys," he said. "Individually you're all right. But when you get together you have all the attributes of a mob."

Mike Aston
Stourbridge, West Midlands

SIR — Most certainly we should honour our forward commitments to the EU. I suggest we use the German system of selecting how one should decide which they are. We should also use the French speed of settlement and the Brussels level of financial probity and regularity of reliable auditing.

Hugh Davy
Thames Ditton, Surrey

SIR — Five years to leave the customs union? We won a war in a shorter time.

Barry Hughes
Lytham St Annes, Lancashire

SIR — If General de Gaulle were still here, he would probably pay us to go.

Martin Bloomfield
Kingston, Surrey

SIR – If we stay in the EU we could have about 60 MEPs and get rid of the rest. The Houses of Parliament could be made into flats.

Bill Smith
Cheam, Surrey

SIR – I voted for Brexit, but the more I hear of the bickering and backstabbing of the MPs of my party and their juvenile and dangerous attempts to be "youthful and popular", together with the insane economic utterances of the Labour party, the more I like the sound of unelected Brussels bureaucrats.

David Wiltshire
Bedford

Barnier storming

SIR – My Remainer friends have become immune to jibes about being a remoaner or a remainiac, but using the expression, "Your pal Barnier . . ." is guaranteed to bring instant outrage.

Peter Miller
Sunninghill, Berkshire

SIR – The EU's Brexit negotiating tactics remind me of a Morecambe and Wise sketch, often repeated. Ernie would take a grip on Eric's shoulder and say "get out of that without moving".

D.P.
Horsham, West Sussex

SIR – Has anyone else noticed the unfortunate aptness of Michel Barnier's surname, with *bar* meaning to prevent or obstruct and *nier* being French for "to deny"?

Peter Ford
Coulsdon, Surrey

SIR – An erudite acquaintance recently introduced me to the word *ineptocracy* in relation to the EU.

My classical education suggests that *kakistocracy* has a more succinct definition.

Richard A.E. Grove
Isle of Whithorn, Wigtownshire

SIR – I have been musing about the New Year's Resolutions Michel Barnier might have jotted on the fly leaf of his diary. The most likely I can come up with is the wisdom of the great Emperor Napoleon Bonaparte: "Never interrupt your enemy while he is making a mistake."

Peter Hall
Marden, Kent

SIR – As a Brexit backup plan, Longwood House on Saint Helena should be redecorated to Mr Barnier's preferred colour scheme.

Gwynne Owen-Smith
Ashford, Kent

SIR – We knew it would have to be a no-deal Brexit when we realised that Mr Barnier uses his middle finger to adjust his glasses.

Andrew Thomas
Malvern, Worcestershire

SIR – Would it help the Brexit negotiations if the main protagonists swapped at half-time? The UK would benefit from Michel Barnier and his team who realise that we are leaving and act accordingly, and the EU would get the lukewarm semi-Remainer leadership which we have endured so far.

Mark Robbins
Bruton, Somerset

Sudden death negotiations

SIR – If Mrs May's team cannot agree a Brexit deal with the EU by March 2019, might I suggest a penalty shoot-out? Suddenly I fancy our chances.

Peter Gale
Oxted, Surrey

SIR – The way things are progressing, the new Brexit mantra should be "Everything is agreed until nothing is agreed".

Anne Grice
London SW14

SIR – Theresa May's red lines now resemble watching butter melt.

Dr Anthony Hawks
Kingston Seymour, Somerset

SIR – It is with good reason that Chequers is referred to as Mrs May's retreat.

Clive More
Maidenhead, Berkshire

SIR – Are Brexit-supporting Ministers who refuse to resign from office now best described as remaining leavers?

Barrington Mumford
Bristol

SIR – Your front-page headline, "Is anyone brave enough to sign May's death warrant?" prompted my wife to respond: "Give me a pen."

A.D. Elworthy
Tiverton, Devon

SIR – A day in the life of a Conservative MP, July 2018.
  7am – Rise.
  7.30am – Take breakfast while reading *The Daily Telegraph*'s Letters page.
  8am – Search for a new job.
  It's not too late for them to do something about it.

Chris Tyrrell
London E1

SIR – I'll bet the Lady's turning now.

Timothy Dyson
Eaton, Nottinghamshire

SIR – Where is Geoffrey Howe when you need him?

C.A. Delahunty
London W2

SIR — Has anyone else noticed that Theresa May walks like a question mark?

Richard Castle
Tetbury, Gloucestershire

SIR — I note that Theresa May is not a quitter. There's the problem.

A.J. Good
Helston, Cornwall

SIR — Isn't that what David Cameron said just before he quit?

Mike West
Eastleigh, Hampshire

SIR — Ted Heath can finally rest easy and stop sulking: the UK now has a Prime Minister even more useless than he was.

Simon Baumgartner
Hampton, Middlesex

SIR — The present political shenanigans bring to mind the supposed Chinese curse, "May you live in interesting times". Or perhaps this should be, "May, you live in interesting times".

Alan Cox
St Clears, Carmarthenshire

SIR — Mrs May has expressed a desire to bring the country together. She is succeeding: more and more voters are against her.

Alan B. Thomas
Warrington, Cheshire

SIR – If Theresa May had been Prime Minister in June 1940:

"We shall make clear our intention to defend our island, within agreed financial limits as set out by the Office for Budget Responsibility; we shall discuss areas of disagreement with our European neighbours on the beaches; we shall conduct impact assessments on the landing grounds; we shall seek parliamentary approval for our negotiating position in the fields and in the streets; we shall convene Cobra in the hills."

> **Kim Thonger**
> Finedon, Northamptonshire

SIR – Hayley Hughes from *Love Island* admits to not having a clue about Brexit, but is Theresa May any better?

> **T. Bradshaw**
> Oxford

SIR – I don't know why the House of Lords has tried to wreck the Brexit process when Mrs May is doing a perfectly good job on her own.

> **Philip J. Honey**
> Retford, Nottinghamshire

SIR – *Once upon a Brexit dreary, as she*
pondered weak and weary.
Over many a difficulty, irritation
and conspiracy.
Suddenly there came a tapping, that
or whispering of sacking.
Multitudes of people laughing,
just outside the PM's door.

Tis just bluster so she muttered
only that and nothing more.
(With apologies to Edgar Allan Poe)

> **John C. Salisbury**
> Mold, Flintshire

SIR – As a former regular at the Coach and Horses (Norman Balon's old pub), I know that his impressive negotiating skills would have achieved an exit by now.

> **Marcus Rowell**
> London SE28

SIR – I suggest a new tactic regarding Brexit.

We should withdraw our request to leave. Vote against or veto every proposal put before the EU parliament. Be generally as obnoxious as Jean-Claude Juncker and the other unelected officials.

After a couple of years they will be begging – and might even pay – us to leave.

> **Jim Bellingall**
> Aylsham, Norfolk

SIR – If we had Donald Trump as Prime Minister, we would have threatened to "nuke" Strasbourg and Brussels, to block the Channel Tunnel and build a wall around Europe by now.

> **Paul Bonner**
> London SW19

SIR — It is clear the only way Mrs May, David Davis and her crew will ever deliver the Brexit the majority of us voted for is to draft in Ross Poldark as a special adviser. He will surely take no nonsense and get things done — with or without his shirt.

Geoff Pringle
Long Sutton, Somerset

SIR — Having just finished *Conclave* by Robert Harris, I would suggest that the Cabinet be locked inside Number 10 until they come up with our Brexit strategy. Smoke signals and a medical team on call for the collection of scalps welcome.

Lamorna Good
Aldeburgh, Suffolk

SIR — Whenever I have kicked a can down the road, it usually goes quite well on the first boot but thereafter it goes wherever it fancies.

Robert Smith
Brentford, Middlesex

SIR — I have a 5,000-piece jigsaw puzzle on my dining room table. I am calmly determined to finish it by March 2019.

Gillian Plowman
Selsey, West Sussex

SIR – I hope that David Davis is keeping in mind just how deceptive these Europeans can be. Only today, I discovered that the European Butter Mountain and Wine Lake are not real. My holiday plans are in ruins.

Hugh Neve
Littlehampton, West Sussex

SIR – How I wish that David Davis would a) threaten to withdraw from negotiations, taking our £40 billion with him; b) drop his rictus grin on emerging from meetings with M. Barnier; and c) stop looking like Julian Assange.

Gordon Brown
Grassington, North Yorkshire

SIR – Why don't we just invade Europe; it's not difficult.

Mark Rayner
Eastbourne, East Sussex

Higher power

SIR – I note with surprise that the Archbishop of Canterbury has called the EU the greatest human achievement "since the fall of the western Roman Empire".

If I were now to criticise the EU publicly – perhaps referring to its inherent inefficiency and corruption – do I risk being defrocked for heresy?

Perhaps the Archbishop could let me know before I write Sunday's sermon.

Fr James Rodley
Harlow, Essex

Older, wiser, more Eurosceptic

SIR – Lord Malloch-Brown stated on the *Today* programme that Britain will become more pro-European as time goes by due to shifting demographics.

This seems at odds with the fact that in 1975 the UK voted overwhelmingly to Remain then reversed that decision 41 years later due to the EU not living up to expectations.

R.K. Hodge
Chichester, West Sussex

SIR – As a pensioner who had the temerity to vote for Brexit, I have become alarmed at the constant reminders of my own mortality.

Recent outbursts about the lack of time I have left before I shuffle off this mortal coil have come from J. Major (75), A. Blair (65) and M. Heseltine (85).

Were Remain voters over 60 given the secret of eternal life? I think we should be told..

R.T. Semain
West Rounton, North Yorkshire

Kein zweites Referendum

SIR – Jürgen Klopp, the manager of Liverpool FC, has said that Britain should have a second vote on Brexit.

He should understand that many of us voted Leave so that we would no longer have to suffer being told what to do by a German.

Roger Smith
Meppershall, Bedfordshire

SIR — In Scotland we have a bath every Hogmanay or referendum, whichever comes first, whether we need it or not.

John Campbell
Lenzie, East Dunbartonshire

SIR — Remainers claim that I was too thick to understand what I was voting for in the Brexit referendum. What makes them think I am now intelligent enough to know what I am voting for if another vote is held on the Brexit deal?

Stephen Keeys
Horsehay, Shropshire

SIR — If Stephen Hawking can say that the complete theory of the universe should, in principle, be understandable by everyone, why is it that Remoaners say that Brexit is too complicated for Brexiteers to comprehend?

If understanding the Universe is easier than understanding how to effect Brexit, then I give up.

Professor R.G. Faulkner
Professor of Physical Metallurgy
Loughborough, Leicestershire

Bottom line

SIR – It is reassuring to know that EU bureaucrats can regulate all parts of our life.

I have just purchased a pack of lavatory paper (made by a company headquartered in Brussels) which informs me – in seven languages – that it is: "Toilet Paper. 100% papermass. Chemical bleached pulp. Total length 22m. Size of a sheet 9.8 x 11cm. 24 x 200 2ply sheets. Net weight 24 x 75g."

My bottom has never before been so well informed. Safe at last from rearguard attack by inferior products.

Natalie Wheen
London SW12

SIR – Whether it is pre- or post-Brexit, I would welcome legislation to agree on a specific colour packet for different flavoured crisps. I am sick of finding a green packet is cheese and onion rather than my intended salt and vinegar.

Michael Smith
Morchard Bishop, Devon

SIR – Is it too much to hope that in March 2019 Brexit will enable us to abandon the totally outdated and purposeless practice of British Summer Time?

Nick Kester
Wattisfield, Suffolk

SIR — I note that a "monster" fatberg blocking a sewer in East London weighs more than ten double decker buses.

Does this mean that post-Brexit the double decker bus may well become the UK unit of mass?

Roger Roue
Canvey Island, Essex

Le passport

SIR — I notice with regret that the contract for the new blue passport looks set to go to a foreign company. However, this frees up British factories to manufacture gunboats, which can then be used for diplomacy. Failing that, they could manufacture quart-pots and furlong rulers.

David Blain
Enfield, Middlesex

SIR — Will the colour of Britain's new passports be described as *sacre bleu*?

Brian Armstrong
North Shields, Tyne and Wear

SIR — Following the passports fiasco, I was wondering whether the government had considered the benefits of outsourcing itself to France.

A.T. Gibbs
Rugby, Warwickshire

SIR — The passport printing crisis can be easily solved. Brexit voters can pay to have their blue passports printed in Britain and the 48 million people who did not vote for

Brexit can choose whether to keep theirs the existing colour. This would make standing in the passport queues far more entertaining.

Dr Chris Keast
Brimpton, Berkshire

The Irish question

SIR – In the published extract from *The Daily Telegraph* from April 1918, it states: "The Irish situation is both grave and menacing." Has nothing changed in a century?

Gregor Gruner
Farnborough, Hampshire

SIR – After Brexit why not monitor the Irish border with a fleet of drones? All-seeing and very soft.

Bernard Crewdson
Maunby, North Yorkshire

SIR – I have often heard it said that if women ruled the world, there would be no wars. I am beginning to doubt this now as the two protagonists involved in Northern Ireland can't sort out a "little local difficulty".

Eric John Harris
Hastings, East Sussex

SIR – As an Ulsterman living in the South of England,
I find that people often try to draw me into a discussion
about Northern Irish politics. My answer is: "It's the best
reason I know for living in Hampshire."

David Robertson
Basingstoke, Hampshire

SIR – There is one way to cure the Ireland/Northern
Ireland border issue: Eire leaving the EU and joining the
UK in an economic union.

At least this could be shortened to Exit.

Colin Robertson
Bramhope, West Yorkshire

Bfree

SIR – It is time the word *Brexit*, freighted as it is with
negativity and lack of direction, is changed to *Bfree* – a
description of positivity and a bright future suitable for a
nation that has so often shown the world the way forward.

Malcolm Parkinson
Sway, Hampshire

SIR – Perhaps the word *Brexit* could become an accepted
swear-word. Then watching debate and news on television
it would be bleeped out, thus providing some much-needed
light entertainment on the whole subject for viewers.

Pauline Kavanagh
Sutton, Surrey

SIR – When watching the BBC news, in the absence of commercial television advertisements, one only has to wait for the word *Brexit* to know that it's a good time to pop out and make a cup of tea.

Bill Hodgman
Gosport, Hampshire

Norway medal model muddle

SIR – Liam Fox said in his Brexit speech: "We are not Canada or Norway."

We figured out that much for ourselves during the last Winter Olympics.

Mark Boyle
Johnstone, Renfrewshire

SIR – During Brexit negotiations, much was made of a Norwegian solution. I failed to realise that meant having our own Quisling in Downing Street.

David Nesbitt
Irthlingborough, Northamptonshire

SIR – I note the sudden interest of our Brexiteer government in "doing great deals" with Canada when, and if, we truly leave the European Union.

I look forward to cheaper maple syrup on my pancakes on Pancake Day.

Nothing else from Canada comes to mind.

Gerald Huxley
Stockport, Cheshire

SIR – A Radio 4 news slot about the Brexit negotiations has just finished.

Four-year-old grandson at the dinner table: "I don't understand why everybody is always talking about breadsticks."

Yvonne Elton
Romsey, Hampshire

Joyous ode

SIR – Having started piano lessons again after 50 years I have succeeded in massacring a very simple version of "Ode to Joy", and have great pleasure in re-naming it "The Brexiteer's Revenge".

Jane Gelder
London SE1

A coalition of correspondents

SIR – I suggest that the next government is formed from your letter-writers, who display more basic common sense on the Brexit issue than the politicians who have clearly failed to deliver what I voted for.

Stuart Duckmanton
Mansfield, Nottinghamshire

Beware the idle March

SIR – I predict that, like many apparently momentous events – joining the EEC, all-day drinking, decimalisation,

VAT, the predicted Y2K computer meltdown, scrapping capital punishment, devolution — what will actually happen on Friday 29 March 2019 is: very little.

Mark Prior
Plymouth, Devon

HOME
THOUGHTS
ON ABROAD

Tit for Vaz

SIR – The wilful deployment of indiscriminate chemical weapons on British soil, spreading lethal toxicity into a peaceful urban area, must be met with a similar, yet more cunning, response. We should replace our ambassador in Moscow with Keith Vaz.

> **Bill Peart**
> Rugby, Warwickshire

SIR – There has been talk of a military-grade nerve agent being used in Salisbury. Are there domestic- or hobby-grade nerve agents?

> **W.H. Statt**
> Swadlincote, Derbyshire

SIR – I hope that the Government remembered to collect all the unpaid parking fines from the Russian diplomats before they were allowed to leave the UK.

> **Tony Cowan**
> Elgin, Moray

SIR – The National Audit Report has declared that Britain is at risk because we are short of experts to combat Cyber warfare.

As Russia is short of intelligence officers in the UK at present, they will appreciate this information.

> **Garry Curran**
> Crowthorne, Berkshire

SIR – Today I spent a good hour on my allotment weeding an area of less than a metre squared.

I thought it may be more appropriate if the world's chemical scientists bent their minds to producing a substance that could kill off bind weed and mare's tail instead of a product that could kill off the world's population.

Roy Deal
Southampton

SIR – Having read of Russia's response to Theresa May's ultimatum, perhaps we need a new word added to our dictionary: *Imputiny*, meaning to do whatever one wishes at any time or place knowing that nobody can touch you for it.

Mike Gibbons
Stradbroke, Suffolk

SIR – Your cartoonist Bob needs to update his drawings of Vladimir Putin to reflect his latest facelift. He looks a lot smoother and more stretched than that now.

Sue Doughty
Twyford, Berkshire

SIR – As Russia is so concerned that Britain may have "abducted" two of their citizens, I propose we send two British citizens to Russia in lieu of the Skripals. Jeremy Corbyn and Diane Abbott both spring to mind as suitable candidates.

Kim Dace
Brenchley, Kent

SIR – Given the stand-off between us and the Russians, it is clear that the UK needs to start fracking immediately.

It's too late when the radiators are cold.

David Chamberlain
Houghton on the Hill, Leicestershire

SIR – It hardly ever snows in Salisbury, yet in March alone we have had two significant snowfalls. Are the Russians to blame for this too?

Steve Maton
Salisbury, Wiltshire

SIR – Various things have made me concerned that "The Russians" are taking over our lives. Firstly, my online grocery order contained items that I am convinced I did not order, then my bicycle computer told me that I'd cycled a lot further than my usual *Telegraph*-collecting ride. I think the Russkies are playing with the satellites.

Ian Mabberley
Abergavenny, Monmouthshire

SIR – I am quite happy for Russia to hack into my computer. All they will find is this email to the *Telegraph*.

Eddie Peart
Rotherham, South Yorkshire

SIR – Readers may be wondering how they can respond to Russia's state-sponsored attempted murder of a former Russian spy and his daughter.

One answer would be never to buy another bottle of Russian vodka. There are some excellent Polish vodkas and

Poland is a great country which never violates international norms.

Richard Snailham
Windsor, Berkshire

SIR – We can only hope that the same person advising Mr Putin that his super new weapons are undetectable is the same person who told him that drug-taking in sport was undetectable.

David Martin
Eyam, Derbyshire

SIR – When considering any sanctions against Russia, Mrs May could perhaps ban Maria Sharapova from Wimbledon.

A couple of years without her screeching would be priceless.

Christopher Mann
Bristol

SIR – If it turns out that Russians are responsible for the attack in Salisbury, Boris Johnson has said he will punish them by refusing to send government officials to the World Cup in the summer.

Oh well, that should frighten the life out of 'em.

Brian Hodgskiss
North Baddesley, Hampshire

SIR – I think England should send a team to the Football World Cup in Russia, but they should play in full chemical protection suits. It might just make a point to Putin and the rest of the world.

David Kirby
Aberystwyth, Ceredigion

A step too far

SIR – Twenty-two-year-old Mamoudou Gassama has been rightly praised for his actions in saving a small child in Paris. It is reported that he had left his home in Mali and travelled through the dangers of sub-Saharan Africa before making a perilous crossing of the Mediterranean. He is now to be made a French citizen.

Hasn't he suffered enough?

Hugh Neve
Littlehampton, West Sussex

Entente trop cordiale

SIR – I wish someone would tell Emmanuel Macron that it isn't really appropriate to maul every head of state he meets.

R.B. Chappell
Saltash, Cornwall

SIR — All President Macron appears to have got from the talks with President Trump is a kiss, a cuddle and his collar felt in the name of dandruff.

Garry Rucklidge
Chapel Allerton, Somerset

SIR — For someone who says he is a germaphobe, President Trump seems to be doing an awful lot of hand holding and dandruff flicking.

Diana M. Jackson
Nether Alderley, Cheshire

SIR — Perhaps the "bromance" between Trump and Macron comes from the similarity in the age differences between them and their wives.

Margaret McCrimmon
St Albans, Hertfordshire

SIR — Theresa May can sleep at night and allay any fears that Monsieur Macron might kiss one cheek too many. Mrs May is quite simply too young for him.

Christopher Learmont-Hughes
Caldy, Wirral

SIR — The mantle of power becomes Mr Macron. He seems to get prettier every time he appears in public.

Liz Saunders
Eastbourne, East Sussex

SIR — My printer is presumably not French, but every time it prints it clearly says: "Macron, Macron, Macron".

David Cullen
Eastbourne, East Sussex

1815 and all that

SIR — Once the conservation work on the Waterloo and Trafalgar paintings in the House of Lords has been completed, I suggest we offer them to the French as the reciprocal loan to the Bayeux Tapestry.

Tom Mullarkey
Ellonby, Cumbria

SIR — Can we please have the parts of France that are rightfully and historically ours. I refer to Normandy, Poitou, Anjou, Gascony, Calais and especially Brittany (it's even got our name on it).

Living by the North Sea, I also notice that the tide goes out every day. We all know where that goes. It must stop. Perhaps we could borrow Donald Trump's wall builders when he has finished his own wall.

Michael Dines
Lowestoft, Suffolk

Governing bigly

SIR — My six-year-old grandson asked me whether I had made a Christmas cake and what was on it.

Yes, I told him, and there were penguins.

"How many penguins?" he asked.

"Eight."

"My cake will have more penguins than that," he said. "And it will have seals as well, and it will be bigger."

Remind you of anyone?

Jennifer Paddock
Sprowston, Norfolk

SIR — We will know that President Trump is serious when he uses our granddaughter's ultimate threat: "You will not be invited to my birthday party."

David Priscott
Lavant, West Sussex

SIR — "Much more humble than you would understand" or "very stable genius" — which is it to be, Mr Trump?

Brian McDowell
Tavistock, Devon

SIR — Now we know that Dr Harold Bornstein's amusingly hyperbolic 2016 report on Donald Trump's health was in effect written by Mr Trump himself, I have another reason to look forward with keen anticipation to reading the President's obituary.

Andrew Mackenzie
Glasgow

SIR — There are two things I do not understand: quantum physics and how Donald Trump is still President.

A.J.C. Gorman
Ickenham, Middlesex

SIR – When you learn that an entrepreneur in the United States has been selling flamethrowers to members of the public, without let or hindrance, you cease to wonder at their choice of President.

Hugh Bebb
Sunbury-on-Thames, Middlesex

Stormy times ahead

SIR – At my age and a little hard of hearing, I was extremely relieved to read that Stormy Daniels was not another weather system but merely a front of a different kind.

Kim Potter
Lambourn, Berkshire

SIR – Whiling away a spare moment, I attempted an anagram of "Stormy Daniels", the porn star suing the President.

All I could come up with was "Money", "Liars" and "STD".

Geoffrey Jarvis
Aboyne, Aberdeenshire

SIR – Your headline quotes Trump stating: "When I make promises, I keep them". I wonder what the text is of the marriage vows in Florida.

Adriaan Stoop
Cardiff

Welcome to Britain, Mr President

SIR — It would appear that Trump's visit to the UK is back on the cards. Great news for the tomato industry.

Robert Fromow
London SW1

SIR — The American President says that "Brits like him a lot". Can we have a referendum on that, please?

Derek Porter
Woking, Surrey

SIR — As President Trump seems so keen on Boris, perhaps he could be persuaded to take him back home with him.

Peter Ferris
Witham, Essex

SIR — If we are to have a trade war with the US, please let us ban the import of Americanisms.

No more *gonna*, no more *wanna* and definitely no *aloominum*.

Anthony Millington
Le Bourdeix, France

SIR — It's really great that Great Britain has such a great relationship with such a great country as America — so much greater than the really great relationships we have with all of the other great countries in our great world.

Oh Lord, give me another adjective.

George Acheson
Fakenham, Norfolk

SIR — The only Prime Minister who has ever had the courage to stand up to the President of the USA is a fictional one played by Hugh Grant in the film *Love Actually*. In Trump-speak: SAD.

Dr Peter Merry
Norwich

SIR — I have always felt that the description of POTUS as "Leader of the Free World" is somewhat offensive, but have never felt strongly enough to voice the opinion.

Given that Trump's policy of "America First" and his infinitely thick orange skin means that he will continue his bullying, narcissistic meander through the organisations and governments that are supposed to be his partners, perhaps we should have a national agreement to stamp out the phrase.

He won't notice, but it will feel good.

Paul Cash
Maidenhead, Berkshire

SIR — It seems that Doughmore Beach in Ireland, where President Trump has his exclusive golf club, is eroding.

How beautifully ironic it would be if he had to build a wall — and pay for it.

Bev Collins
Droitwich Spa, Worcestershire

SIR — We are told that President Trump is teetotal. Might things be diplomatically more straightforward if he were not?

Patrick Maclure
Winchester

SIR — Trump is said to be tired of Theresa May's "school mistress" tone.

Perhaps he hasn't noticed that the rest of the world is exasperated by his "schoolboy" tone.

Sheila Robertson
London W11

SIR — It appears that Mr Trump is making America grate again.

Martin Bloomfield
Kingston upon Thames, Surrey

Fringe benefits

SIR — On reading about Donald Trump's expensive treatment for hair loss, I might have a solution: get someone to whack him on the head. Last year I sustained a head injury just inside the hairline. A few months later new hair started to grow and I am now sporting a very nice new fringe.

Julia Wilson
Rainham, Kent

SIR — Why is it that President Trump, who comes from the land of the free — also the land of the (mainly) natural looking toupee and rug — won't avail himself of his country's expertise?

Wilma Haley
Doncaster, Yorkshire

SIR – Does Airforce One have a tanning machine?

Ian McKenzie
Pavenham, Bedfordshire

SIR – Surely the best thing Donald Trump could do would be to have a sponsored head shave.

It could raise millions for charity and allow the world to see him in a more positive light – for now.

Garry Gibson
Jedburgh, Roxburghshire

When Donald met Kim

SIR – Donald Trump and Kim Jong-un: unstoppable farce meets immovable despot?

Charles Janz
London SW14

SIR – What might the diplomatic gifts be between the men who want everything?

C.J. Fletcher
Stanton St John, Oxfordshire

SIR – I wonder if, in the interests of world peace, somebody could persuade Twitter to delete President Trump's account.

John Wilson
North Cadbury, Somerset

SIR – I wonder if there is any provision in the Agreement signed between Donald Trump and Kim Jong-Un for a hotel and golf course to replace the dismantled and destroyed North Korea nuclear sites, with the craters to be used as bunkers.

Josh Cosnett
Oxted, Surrey

SIR — Does Donald Trump do his oversize signature with a felt pen because they don't allow him sharp objects?

Bruce Cochrane
Bridge of Allan, Stirling

America's gunfight

SIR — When the last two Americans shoot each other dead, the country will get the message. Too late, alas.

Richard Statham
Langport, Somerset

SIR — Americans can keep their guns as long as they ban ammunition.

Jan Bardey
Kineton, Warwickshire

SIR — Good thing they don't have knives in America; otherwise it will look like a war zone.

Howard Boughtflower
Princes Risborough, Buckinghamshire

SIR — A colleague at the school I work at has devised the absorbing game of "Which five staff should we arm?"

It is a deeply engrossing game and has caused lively debate around the building among staff and pupils.

I recommend it to all workplaces as an interesting digression.

Noeleen Murphy
London SE22

SIR — I can just imagine my grumpy old history teacher in his dusty robes with a Glock on his hip. He was dangerous enough with a blackboard rubber. He would have shot the whole class before lunchtime.

Graham Masterton
Tadworth, Surrey

Syrian de-fence

SIR — I had been undecided about what action we should take in Syria, if any, but now that I hear Tony Blair is advocating direct intervention, I've suddenly come down off the fence.

Alan Eastwood
Knutsford, Cheshire

SIR — If we attack Syria, will our bombs be nice, kind, democracy-producing bombs, like the ones we used in Iraq, Afghanistan and Libya?

Dr Christopher Madoc-Jones
Denbigh

SIR — Would it not be more effective, as a direct deterrent to Assad, and more acceptable to many than the destruction of equipment and other people's lives, simply to spray indelible ink over his palatial complex?

Imagine the inconvenience, the worldwide ridicule and ignominy.

Chris Williams
Adlington, Cheshire

SIR — We have learnt that four RAF planes took part in the bombing of Syria.

Unfortunately, due to the recent defence spending review, it's likely this was the entire RAF.

Joe MacVeigh
Romford, Essex

Aw-gag-nanm

SIR — I regret the downfall of President Mugabe because I could always remember his name as E-ba-gum backwards. Mnangagwa is difficult to remember forwards or backwards.

Frank Hill
Malvern, Worcestershire

Then in Rome

SIR — Back in the 1930s, Mussolini once said, "It's not impossible to govern Italy, merely pointless."

It seems not a lot has changed.

Roger Chappell
Allesley, Warwickshire

Charity away from home

SIR — I was stunned to hear of Oxfam employees paying for prostitutes.

When I was manager of an Oxfam shop I was earning £3.60 an hour.

How on earth could they afford them?

M. Bowman
Shrewsbury, Shropshire

SIR — The news of the Oxfam scandal has a similar effect for most people as learning that one's revered grandmother has been charged with shoplifting.

Brian Checkland
Thingwall, Wirral

Global goodbyes

SIR — Some 20 years ago I found myself in a multinational group of people parting company on a busy street corner in Paris. There were English, French, Germans, Australians and Japanese in the group. The French kissed everyone on both cheeks; the Germans shook hands; the Australians slapped everyone on the back; the Japanese bowed; and the English stood around looking bemused.

I often wonder how the resulting pantomime appeared to passers-by.

Sally Gibbons
London SW19

Parlez-vous Franglais?

SIR — There is an obvious solution for the French concerning their problems with Franglais — opt for English as their primary language.

Comme ça — or "sorted", as they may say in the new vernacular.

John R.M. Prime
Havant, Hampshire

SIR — Could there be a use at last for Esperanto as the official language of the anticipated European military?

William Fisher
Hungerford, Berkshire

Dish of the day

SIR — While lunching in France during a year abroad over 30 years ago with a fellow language student (who was American), he asked the waiter in his limited French for "un doggy bag" for the remains of his rather large steak.

Looking puzzled, the waiter went away, and came back later with a parcel wrapped in newspaper.

It contained bones for a dog.

Margarete Isherwood
Leamington Spa, Warwickshire

SIR — Nick Timothy is right to suggest that everyone who resides in this country should at least speak the language. However, there are many Britons living and retired in places like Spain who use English in a loud voice to get by, and if that doesn't work, shout.

Imagine a Pakistani or Polish person trying that method in Tesco over here.

Michael Sarling
Braintree, Essex

SIR – Language problems certainly made a dinner at a restaurant in Rome extremely expensive. We were delighted to have the attention of the friendly effusive owner.

"Have this on the house?" he kept asking about successive dishes.

Of course we agreed.

When the enormous bill arrived we discovered that "On the house" really meant "House speciality".

Danny Koffman
London NW4

SIR – A Dutch airline pilot once told me that "Dutch is not a language, more of a throat infection".

Mary Baker
Henham, Hertfordshire

THE USE AND
ABUSE OF
LANGUAGE

Keyboard worrier

SIR — Having just received the third work email of the day starting "I hope you're well?" I need advice.

Should I tell the sender how I am? Should I reply, pointing out the stray question mark? Or should I sigh, mutter and respond to the email with the lingering feeling that somehow I am missing the opportunity to go into full Victor Meldrew mode?

Or is it possible that no one else cares?

Steven Broomfield
Eastleigh, Hampshire

Monsieur Le General n'est pas chez lui

SIR — I am sure it is right to ban cold call centres based both here and overseas. However, I shall miss answering in one of my many guises — from being a grumpy retired French general to being an excited Italian diplomat and speaking in the smattering I possess of their mother tongues. Such great, free entertainment will come to an end.

Ron Kirby
Dorchester, Dorset

SIR — Notifying a motor insurer of change of address:
    Me: "Bexhill hyphen on hyphen Sea."
    Call centre: "How do you spell hyphen?"

Denis Durkin
Bexhill-on-Sea, East Sussex

SIR – If I get one more email this October containing the phrase "spooktacular deals", I am going to go out and bite somebody.

James Bibby
Prenton, Wirral

Word search

SIR – Where on earth, or in the waters under it, may I find a cod with an accent?

Chris Spurrier
Eversley, Hampshire

SIR – Is there any other daylight apart from broad?

Judith Manderioli
London W13

SIR – How does a pause become pregnant, and how long is the gestation period?

B. Leonard
Cardiff

SIR – Should it not be grocers' apostrophe rather than grocer's?
    After all, lots of them do it.

Michael Cheetham
Hurstpierpoint, West Sussex

SIR – What's the difference between modern emoji and Egyptian hieroglyphs?

> **Paul Spencer**
> Thame, Oxfordshire

SIR – Back in the old days, no one said *back in the day*.

> **Martin Burgess**
> Beckenham, Kent

SIR – Why is it that Cabinet members are reshuffled while a pack of cards is simply shuffled?

> **Dick Raffety**
> Chew Stoke, Somerset

SIR – Given the closure or reduced opening hours of many high-street banks, is it still appropriate for there to be bank holidays?

> **Sue Gresham**
> Holt, Norfolk

SIR – Can "anecdotal evidence" include talking to oneself?

> **Peter Walton**
> Wilmslow, Cheshire

SIR – One of my sons phoned today and said he'd just had a long "oneversation" with his youngest sister. Fellow listeners won't require any explanation.

> **Kevin Heneghan**
> St Helens, Lancashire

The Irish question

SIR – My confusion over the Irish border negotiations is compounded by the fact that whenever an Ulster politician or correspondent says *whenever*, they actually mean *when*. "Whenever Theresa May comes to Belfast" doesn't mean she is a regular visitor and may actually mean she hasn't yet visited at all.

Can I humbly suggest that Northern Ireland adopts the word *when* like the rest of the world?

Keith Valentine
Tunbridge Wells, Kent

Clock wisdom

SIR – One useful spin-off from learning to read a clock face is the concept of clockwise or anticlockwise, expressed in a single English word.

For example, the French for "anticlockwise" is "dans le sens inverse des aiguilles d'une montre".

I wonder how they translate the title of John Cleese's film.

Arnold Burston
Burton-on-Trent, Staffordshire

SIR – Had my eight-year-old daughter not understood instructions using the concepts of clockwise and anticlockwise, she would still now be stuck in a toilet in Austria.

Valerie Atkin
Sheffield

Thyme servers

SIR – Driving past Ford prison today I saw that the inmates have renamed their farm shop. It's now called "Serving Thyme".

Philip Moger
East Preston, West Sussex

SIR – The former wife of a football coach who posted a full English breakfast through his letterbox was sentenced to a 12-month community order. She should do porridge.

R. Allan Reese
Dorchester, Dorset

SIR – You report on a barrister who is suing his firm over a spanking session with a colleague on office premises. He was apparently suspended some months after the incident and with no trace of irony complained to a legal website about "disciplinary proceedings" brought against him.

No doubt he enjoyed them.

Ian Prideaux
London SW4

Carillion regardless

SIR – Which bright spark thought it was a good idea to use a corruption of "carrion" and "ill" as the name of a public company?

John Curran
Bristol

SIR – I was very sorry to hear of the demise of that national chain of stores. I shall now always think of it as "Toysaurus".

Jeremy Douglas-Jones
Swansea

Embarrassing emphases

SIR – Many people complain that they have been in some way har*assed* – with the accent on the second syllable. None of them appear to be emba*rrassed* (with the accent on the third syllable) by so doing.

I find this strange. I also think that Michael Crawford, playing Cornelius Hackl in the film *Hello, Dolly!*, has a lot to answer for.

Terry Whiting
Lincoln

SIR – I suggest the re-emergence of the word *unbecoming* as an alternative to *inappropriate*. This charming word brings to mind the film *Conduct Unbecoming*. Both the storyline and the title would be most pertinent in today's age of #MeToo.

Jonathan Dart
Sherborne, Dorset

SIR – If Harvey Wein*stine* pronounces his name Wine*steen*, does that mean that German beer is now served in a *steen*? And what about Alfred Ein*stine*?

I just wish someone would make a definitive ruling on this because I'm getting awfully confused.

Robert Paterson
Speen, Berkshire

SIR — Pronunciation is a useful means of differentiating between the inhabitants of this modest seaside town. Those who say Sea*ford* are intelligent locals; those who say *Sea*ford are ignorant invaders.

Diana Crook
Seaford, East Sussex

SIR — Can we add *staycation* to the growing list of language abominations?

Geoff Pursglove
Snarestone, Leicestershire

Sweet talk

SIR — A Virgin Trains passenger has complained about being addressed by staff as "Honey". She'd better stay clear of Devon. During a recent telephone conversation with the proprietrix of a Dartmouth pet shop, I was addressed as "My lover".

I was delighted.

George S. Pearson
Southsea, Hampshire

SIR — Some time ago my elder brother came to assist me in a loft clearing job. He had borrowed a Ford Mondeo for the task. We made regular visits to the council tip. I was driving my Mercedes.

During our second of many visits we realised that I was addressed as *Governor* and he as *Mate*.

Anthony Scouller
Banstead, Surrey

SIR – In my 79th year I am frequently patronised as "love". I have found that my reply, "Bless you my child", makes a point, and at the same I accept the well-meant greeting.

Revd Keith Horsfall
Swaffham, Norfolk

SIR – I have a fairly deep voice and am frequently perceived to be a man when on the phone, usually getting called Sir.

On saying to one man, "It is Madam, actually", the reply was, "Sorry, love".

Grrrrr.

Jan Reeks
Gloucester

Hello, boys (and girls)

SIR – Given that one can now be censured for "misgendering" an individual, can I now complain when, in a group of both men and women, I am greeted with the term, "Hello guys"?

Jennifer Franklin
Pontefract, West Yorkshire

SIR – Celia Walden rightly baulks at the Shadow Chancellor's use of the term "fisherpeople". I wonder when, so as not to cause offence, Mr McDonnell will refer to "the taxperson".

Tim Matthews
London N6

SIR – It's a good job the Apostle Peter didn't take Jesus literally when told he'd been made "a fisher of men", otherwise no women would have been saved for us (saved) chaps.

J. Eric Nolan
Wilpshire, Lancashire

SIR – You report that Oxford academics are asked to use writers' first names, rather than initials, "to make it clearer which are female".

How are they to cite George Sand and Evelyn Waugh?

Prof. Rennie McElroy
Carlops, Peeblesshire

SIR – If boys wearing skirts becomes the norm, isn't there a very real danger that the expression "to de-bag" will disappear from the English language?

Jasper Archer
Stapleford, Wiltshire

SIR – With the need to adopt gender-neutral language, I am at a loss as to how, in future, I should state my name.

B.D. Chapman
Sidmouth, Devon

Nothing like a dame

SIR – With the publication of the New Year Honours List many of us are, once again, struck with the ridiculousness of this title of "Dame" and its connotation of pantomimes and Widow Twankey, while citizens of other countries use the word as a semi-derogatory term.

Any suggestions anyone?

David Gunn
Shipston-on-Stour, Warwickshire

SIR – One hundred years after suffrage, women should rebel against the repellent label "feisty". It derives from the Middle English verb "to break wind", which was so regularly applied to small dogs that "feist" became a term for a snappy lap-dog: dogs with flatulence were commonly believed to be more aggressive.

Caroline Moore
Etchingham, East Sussex

SIR – Your editorial today must have been written by a bloke because it showed a shocking lack of precision concerning the female pudenda.

"Vulvas?" Even with my O-level Latin, failed three times, I know it should be *vulvae*.

It all reminded me of that A.P. Herbert poem:

That part of a woman's anatomy
That most appeals to Man's depravity
Is constructed with considerable care
And what appears to be a common little cavity
Is really an elaborate affair.

I could go on but don't want to frighten old brigadiers over their brekkie.

Rosemary Foster
Angmering, West Sussex

Teaching the one R

SIR — I'll tell you why we need grammar schools. This morning Radio 4 talked to two teachers, one of whom announced: "Our school has children between eleven to sixteen; I teach them English."

Brenda Frisby
Cottesmore, Rutland

SIR — We don't need any weird "reading revolution"; just leave the cornflakes packet on the breakfast table. I was quite fluent in the early 1930s after a year or two of Post Toasties.

Tim Topps
Oxford

SIR — My father was called "cheerfully incompetent" in a report by one of his teachers. He became a highly successful corporate finance director for Midland Bank and I am pleased to say that he remained cheerful throughout his career.

Pauline Lucas
Southend-on-Sea, Essex

SIR — I well remember one master writing in my end of year report, "John remains as incorrigible and enigmatic as ever."

At the time he was, thankfully, blissfully unaware that I had recently seduced his daughter.

J.W.
Driffield, East Yorkshire

SIR – If the handwriting of the nation's children is as bad as they say it is, there should be no problem filling all the vacant NHS medical posts when they graduate.

David J. Hartshorn
Badby, Northamptonshire

Tricky pill to swallow

SIR – I have sometimes suspected that the naming of new, invariably polysyllabic, drugs is achieved by selecting quantities of consonants and vowels more or less at random.

The latest among these, *Canakinumab*, becomes infinitely more memorable if read backwards.

Dr Lawrence Green
Langley, Warwickshire

SIR – The failure of the contraceptive pill among first-time users is probably a direct result of the BBC's repeated references to the *aural* contraceptive. Dangerous too, as pills are difficult to remove from the ear.

Malcolm Shifrin
Leatherhead, Surrey

SIR – In the 1970s my wife was working on an ENT ward where a trainee nurse was told to give a patient two suppositories. A little later these were removed from the patient's ears and popped into the correct orifice with better results.

Robert Hurlow FRCS
Marnhull, Dorset

SIR – If "spotted dick" is to be relegated to being solely a dermatological entity, must "cock-a-leekie", likewise, become a term confined entirely to urological practice?

David Abell
Portsmouth

SIR – When I was a publican I always told my patients that I had the best surgery in the village.

Prescriptions were relatively inexpensive and 95 per cent of people went away happier than when they arrived.

David Smith
Cudworth, Somerset

Money for nothing

SIR – I am constantly reading signs on "holes in the wall" that offer "free cash" – and yet when I use them to withdraw cash my bank account gets debited.

Surely this is a case of blatant misrepresentation?

Linda Lewin
Teddington, Middlesex

SIR – A small van passed me yesterday bearing the legend: "Making tomorrow a better place". I think they'll need a bigger vehicle.

Tim Nicholson
Cranbrook, Kent

SIR – Since retiring I have lived very happily in a bungalow. Or at least I thought I had. A local estate agent is offering a dwelling very similar to mine which is described as a "single-storey house".

I await with interest the appearance of a two-storey bungalow.

D. Hodgkiss
Cranleigh, Surrey

SIR – I was intrigued by the report suggesting that the terms "drug addict" and "junkie" should be replaced by a reference to the person having a "heroin use disorder".

I'm wondering whether burglars will be described as someone having a "property ownership confusion disorder".

Malcolm Allsop
Wroxham, Norfolk

War of words

SIR – I should have more faith in the sombre warnings of General Sir Nick Carter if he could accurately pronounce the word *nuclear*.

Ged Martin
Youghal, County Cork, Ireland

SIR – Now that the letter H is pronounced *Haitch*, should we refer to Y as *Yigh*?

James Stevenson
Kingsbridge, Devon

SIR – Let's just give in and agree. The second month of the year is *Febry*.

Dr P.E. Pears
Coleshill, Warwickshire

SIR – Is it an Americanism to refer to a stroke in a sentence as a *slash*?

In my book, the latter is a basic bodily function.

Nevill Swanson
Worcester

SIR – The late Jim Bowen may have uttered 43 *smashin*'s in half an hour, but he is put in the shade by a young American man I once overheard in the pub. He managed to squeeze the word *like* into a conversation 15 times in just 20 seconds.

Seán Bellew
London W12

SIR – How does one explain to someone trying to learn the English language that, after cutting a tree down, we then cut it up?

Chris Cansdale
Latimer, Buckinghamshire

SIR – Many people seem to be *filling out* forms these days. Whatever happened to *filling in*?

Peter McPherson
Merriott, Somerset

SIR – The words *floor* and *ground* seem to have become interchangeable. Should I have the misfortune to fall over, the floor would be a preferable surface as it may be carpeted.

Valerie Hogg
Glasgow

SIR – As well as changes in the meaning of some English words, I've noticed new meanings for acronyms. STD was Subscriber Trunk Dialling; PMT Potteries Motor Traction (a large 'bus company); and AI was Artificial Insemination.

Arnold Burston
Rolleston on Dove, Staffordshire

SIR – Good luck to Velcro with their beautifully polite attempt to deter others from using their brand name as a generic. Hoover and Biro didn't have much luck.

Sandra Hawke
Andover, Hampshire

SIR – Woodbridge Town Council has announced new signage in an attempt to "badge our assets".

I believe Adam and Eve did something similar with fig leaves.

Michael Hughes
Wickham Market, Suffolk

SIR – Surely everyone now realises there is no noun that cannot be verbed.

Emeritus Professor Geoff Moore
Millport, Ayrshire

SIR – I'm always proud when I have lettered in *The Daily Telegraph*.

Andrew Holgate
Poynton, Cheshire

Back to basics

SIR – Have I really just witnessed Fraser Nelson, one of the best political journalists in the country, using the term "revert back" in today's edition? If he was quoting a Dutchman then he is forgiven.

Brian Wilson
Glasgow

SIR – I was sat at breakfast yesterday reading *The Daily Telegraph* and my wife was stood next to me.

We are both horrified by this popular abomination of the English language but have decided to join in just to annoy ourselves.

Mark Stephens
Hungerford, Berkshire

The two Ronnies

SIR – Who are the "two Rons" that the weather forecasters and newscasters at the BBC keep alluding to? Every day they keep mentioning "Later Ron" and "Earlier Ron", but there is never a mention of who they are or where they reside.

Derek Partner
Chiddingfold, Surrey

SIR – We're often told that snow and ice will be treacherous. How so? As far as I am aware, they owe allegiance to no one.

Andrew Blake
Shalbourne, Wiltshire

SIR – Scottish place names are quite wonderful things for faux swear words.

Following the weather forecast, having seen some of the lesser-known settlements throughout Scotland appearing on our screens, we are tempted from time to time to utter something about Socialist *Fochabers*, or that *Ecclefechan* Jeremy Corbyn (or Nicola Sturgeon).

However, we avoid using *Unst*, as it is simply too rude.

Andrew H.N. Gray
Edinburgh

Hello, this is the BBC

SIR – BBC Radio Four seems to have abandoned "Good morning/afternoon/evening" in favour of the gratuitously informal "Hello".

They should never have got rid of dinner jackets.

Joseph B. Fox
Redhill, Surrey

SIR – Is there a competition to find the fastest-talking speaker on the BBC?

Joyce Whitfield
Wirral

SIR – According to the BBC, the police force has been replaced by *the pleece*.

M. Hely
Banham, Norfolk

SIR – Has anyone else noticed the stealthy appearance of a new television channel called *BBC Toe*?

> **Paul Machin**
> Cheltenham, Gloucestershire

SIR – Is anyone else irritated by being ordered to "relax" on Classic FM?

> **Dr Peter I. Vardy**
> Runcorn, Cheshire

SIR – I was amused to see on BBC Breakfast television this morning an interview with a Cromer fisherman wearing a T-shirt upon which was printed *Aaaah – Soles*. Fortunately this was not spotted by the BBC.

> **John Grandy**
> Bourton, Dorset

SIR – An enjoyable distraction at my gym is reading subtitles generated by speech recognition software. I have seen them identify leading politicians such as: "A mandible Macaroon"; "Ahmed-in-a-dinner-jacket"; and "Barack, a bomber".

> **Antony Thomas**
> Esher, Surrey

SIR – On Wednesday's BBC News "the Prime Minister's top lieutenants" became "the Prime Minister's topless tenants".

> **Eugene Harkin**
> Bolton, Lancashire

THAT'S ENTERTAINMENT?

They all play in a blue submarine

SIR – The picture of the submersible used to photograph the deeps of the ocean on *Blue Planet* does seem rather small. Just where do they put the orchestra that seems to accompany them everywhere?

Robert Ward
Loughborough, Leicestershire

Everyday story of intergalactic folk

SIR – I have just listened to *The Hitchhiker's Guide to the Galaxy* followed by *The Archers*. I noticed no difference in the plot.

Cenydd Thomas
Brecon

SIR – Can anyone tell me why the producers of *The Archers* bother with an agricultural adviser? He must be exceedingly bored.

Jane Bell
Belmaduthy, Ross-shire

SIR – Hooray for a new editor for *The Archers*. Let's hope he, too, hasn't got a baby obsession, as the last few weeks of the programme have been saturated with baby scans, baby classes and surrogate babies to such a degree that I might have to take maternity leave and switch off.

Jane Wood
Tisbury, Wiltshire

One killed every minute

SIR – First we lose Nic on *The Archers* to sepsis, then Barbara from *Call the Midwife* in a similar vein.

I dare not move anywhere near Oxford, East Anglia, Jersey, London, Manchester, Birmingham, Shetland or the Caribbean for fear of getting murdered.

John Robert Dalton
Middle Woodford, Wiltshire

Knives out

SIR – My wife and I have a new game which is to see if we can spot any actor in a modern drama who uses a knife at all. So far we have failed. They all use a fork only as a shovel.

J. Mills
Casterton, Cumbria

Portillo's poker face

SIR – Michael Portillo would make an excellent poker player. Week after week, he manages to conceal his distaste for the flamboyant colour combinations that he is asked to wear on *Great British Railway Journeys*.

Bruce Ridge
Clevedon, North Somerset

SIR – I fail to understand why there is so much fuss concerning train services and the railways in this country. I regularly watch Michael Portillo on television and he does not seem to experience any difficulty. Much of the time he is the only person in a carriage. Perhaps he is the man to put in charge to sort out any problems?

Roger Noons
Kingswinford, West Midlands

Artists above their station

SIR – One often hears the question "What is art?" whenever the contentious issue of contemporary art is discussed. On seeing the photograph of Tracey Emin's latest installation at St Pancras Station, I could perhaps ask: What isn't art?

Shaun Whyte
Alnmouth, Northumberland

Ant on the skids

SIR – I note that Ant McPartlin was fined £86,000 for drink-driving. With a reported weekly salary of £130,000, I'm relieved to know that Mr McPartlin had £44,000 left to last him until the end of the week.

Wg Cdr Kevin Dowling (retd)
Welbourn, Lincolnshire

SIR – At least now I know which is Ant and which is Dec.

Pam Lyons
Holywell, Flintshire

Literal putdown

SIR – Has anyone apart from Mr Booker ever read a book by Salman Rushdie?

Richard Youens
Pewsey, Wiltshire

Lost in translation

SIR — *McMafia* almost justifies the TV licence as it is gripping to watch.

What I like best is the look on James Norton's face as he wishes he understood Russian.

Charlotte Joseph
Lawford, Essex

Custard and jelly revenge

SIR — We now have an Oscar nomination for a Briton who plays his part with a faultless American accent. Is this payback time for Dick Van Dyke in *Mary Poppins*?

John Rowlands
Harpenden, Hertfordshire

SIR — My husband wants to be known as the man who never saw *The Sound of Music*.

Ann Garbett
Sheffield

SIR — If the actress playing Maria in *West Side Story* must come from Puerto Rico, who is to play Titania in *A Midsummer Night's Dream*?

She hails from Fairyland.

Andrew Lakeman
Pensford, Somerset

SIR — I look forward to a new production of Wagner's Ring Cycle using real live giants.

Rosie Clarke
Nailsea, North Somerset

Hopping mad

SIR — I was heartened to read that Allergy UK is seeking the withdrawal of the Peter Rabbit film, in which a rabbit pelts a deadly enemy with berries to which he is allergic.

I was going to complain about the portrayal of a white male authority figure mistreating weaker creatures.

They have saved me a stamp.

Margaret Ellis
High Bentham, North Yorkshire

Humphrys in the hot seat

SIR — I am surprised anyone can support the BBC paying John Humphrys some £600,000 for skewering the slippery and disingenuous when most of us would be happy to do it for free.

Michael Edwards
Haslemere, Surrey

SIR — Of course Demelza shouldn't get the same pay as Ross Poldark. He gallops a horse along a cliff edge, goes down dangerous mines, scythes grass and fights everyone.

She sits at home feeling peeved and has an affair with a short-sighted naval officer.

Malcolm Allen
Berkhamsted, Hertfordshire

The Ten O'Clock Maybe

SIR – The BBC News is known in our household as the "Could, Should, Might and Maybe half hour".

When will presenters cease to offer their opinions and report fact?

Martin Sobey
Dartmouth, Devon

SIR – You know the summer holidays are finally over when BBC News is no longer a Laura Kuenssberg-free zone.

Stephen Howey
Woodford Green, Essex

SIR – How do TV producers decide which items of news should be presented standing and which sitting?

John Mayo
Hewelsfield, Gloucestershire

SIR – I have noticed that on television chat shows there is now a tendency to remain seated when shaking hands. This, along with military saluting without a hat, is likely to incur the wrath of God.

Chris Harding
Parkstone, Dorset

Million dollar question

SIR — How can anyone who has watched *Who Wants to Be a Millionaire?* still support our state-sector comprehensive education system?

Brian Christley
Abergele, Conwy

The sacking of Troy

SIR — Last night I watched part of the final episode of the BBC's *Troy: Fall of a City*. The production was on a lavish enough scale but the dialogue was ruinous to the overall effect. An ill-chosen phrase here, or a supererogatory word there, made it all sound a little too colloquially modern and quite out of place.

Now that the city has been sacked, a like fate ought to befall the scriptwriter.

Derrick Gillingham
London SW1

Fighting talk

SIR — I was settling down this evening to watch the boxing match for the WBC world flyweight eliminator when Channel 5 announced that "the following programme may contain scenes of violence".

Well, you could have knocked me down with a feather duster.

Dave I'Anson
Formby, Merseyside

GOOD AND BAD SPORTS

An Englishman, two Kiwis and a Scotsman

SIR – Tribalism in sport is real. My wife and I happened to be in Madeira on holiday for the Rugby World Cup final in 2003 and were watching the match in a bar with two New Zealanders, a Scotsman and a South African.

Being English, my wife and I were supporting England. The Scot was supporting Australia, as he clearly could not cheer on England. The New Zealanders were supporting England as they clearly could not support Australia, and the South African was supporting whoever was winning at the time.

Richard Packer
Westcott, Surrey

Crocodile tears

SIR – It could just be me but, frankly, I am more disappointed in the Australian cricketers for the tears than the ball tampering.

Judith A. Scott
St Ives, Cambridgeshire

SIR – The weeping and wailing by the Aussies is not really part of their psyche. Have any of the TV cameras picked up the surreptitious use of peeled onions?

Peter Williams
Rufforth, North Yorkshire

SIR – Surely one way to stop cheating on the cricket pitch is to remove pockets from the cricket trousers.

Why do they need trouser pockets on the cricket pitch?

Mike Maloney
St Albans, Hertfordshire

SIR — A new cricket ball with one side pre-roughened could solve a problem.

Thomas Wilkinson
Filey, North Yorkshire

SIR — It's bad enough the Australians are beating us at the cricket, but now they're sending us their flu.

Nick Mawer
Eastbourne, East Sussex

SIR — I fail to be surprised by the behaviour of the Australian cricket team. After all, we sent their families out there in prison ships.

David J. Hartshorn
Badby, Northamptonshire

SIR — At last! Some cricket coverage in *The Daily Telegraph*.

Elizabeth Bellamy
Cleethorpes, Lincolnshire

Broken boundaries

SIR — Trying to find an edible avocado at a supermarket, I muttered crossly: "You could play cricket with these."

Another avocado-seeker, a delightful Indian gentleman, offered from over my left shoulder: "England couldn't."

At the time, England were touring India and were under

the cosh. We adjourned to the in-store cafe for coffee, over
which we shared our love, and then went our separate ways.

Anne Jappie
Cheltenham, Gloucestershire

Gentlemanly players

SIR – Back in the mists of time the English cricket team was
comprised of "Players" and "Gentlemen". We may think
that we live in more democratic and enlightened times but
at least back then the "Players" were also gentlemen.

David Salter
Kew, Surrey

SIR – What is the world coming to? Two young men were
shown drinking Prosecco, from plastic glasses, at Lords, on
day three of the test match.

Garth McGowen
Littleport, Cambridgeshire

No guide to future (enhanced) performance

SIR – If professional sports people are spot-tested and
punished for recreational drug-taking then why are those
who look after our pensions and investments not also spot-
tested?

Richard Tinn
Boston, Lincolnshire

SIR — I think we can safely assume that the England cricket team will not be accused of using any performance-enhancing substances.

Nick Cudmore
Grimoldby, Lincolnshire

SIR — I now feel conscience-bound to admit that I was given a glucose tablet half an hour before I ran the 100 yards in the District Sports in 1957.

Should I return my silver medal to the district schools' authority?

Rita Russell
Lingfield, Surrey

A game of six clichés

SIR — Not being much of a linguist, I've spent the off-season learning Premiership-speak.

I've put together a few words and phrases that may assist the uninitiated to more fully understand the game:

Unbelievable — quite good
Outstanding — not bad
Superb — average
A difficult skill to master — can't kick with his left foot
Went down easily — cheated
He's really hurt — he's a cry-baby.

I hope that helps.

Phil Roberts
Melton Mowbray, Leicestershire

SIR — Just when we thought that the word *turgid* had been dropped from the sporting vocabulary it popped up again over the festive period.

A commentator on Radio 4 described the cricket pitch at Melbourne as *turgid*.

This is when my brain went into overdrive trying to picture this cricket pitch, bearing in mind that the two terms used in sex education at school many years ago were "flaccid" and "turgid" to describe the state of a certain part of the anatomy.

John Hewett
Ponteland, Northumberland

SIR — Eddie Jones has shown, once again, that he is a grand-master of *testiculation*: the art of waving one's arms around aimlessly while talking a lot of balls.

Philip Richards
Castletown, Isle of Man

Fore!

SIR — The curse of slow play in golf would be alleviated if the laws were changed to allow tackling.

Phil Saunders
Bungay, Suffolk

Thugby vs yob-ball

SIR — My rugby-loving friends, including myself, refer to football as "yob-ball". Our football-supporting friends refer to rugby as "thugby".

Philip Samengo-Turner
Cirencester, Gloucestershire

SIR – Our games master, Dai Roberts, couldn't bring himself to say either "football" or "soccer". He used to refer to it as "the game with the round ball", and woe betide any of us boys caught playing it.

David Smith
Calverton, Nottinghamshire

Wearing one's nose on one's sleeve

SIR – I read that Arsenal is looking to get sleeve sponsorship. May I suggest Kleenex for Arsène Wenger's, as he never seems to have a hankie when he needs one.

David James
Tavistock, Devon

SIR – Following Arsenal Football Club, as I do, is about as relaxing as being a Jesuit in Elizabethan England.

Mike Humphries
Barton-on-Sea, Hampshire

Weekly pay packet

SIR – Why is it that the pay of football players is almost always referred to in terms of weekly wages? I can think of no other profession where the professional's pay is quoted in anything other than an annual figure.

It is common to hear that a player is getting £100,000 a week but you never hear that the Prime Minister is on a rather piffling, by comparison, £3,000 a week.

Nicholas Cooper
Dartmouth, Devon

Hole in run

SIR — While watching the London Marathon I realised that, whichever stretch of road was being televised, I had not seen one pothole.

Now I know why there is not a Cumbrian Marathon — the potholes are knee-deep around here.

Shirley J. Ramshaw
Arnside, Cumbria

SIR — Catching a glimpse of the London Marathon as I was channel-hopping reminded me of my favourite oxymoron: fun-run.

Clive Hallett
Wheatley, Oxfordshire

Walk-on parts in darts

SIR — News that the Professional Darts Corporation will cease the practice of "walk-on girls" accompanying the players at the start of the match is concerning.

Surely these gentlemen can't be expected to find the dart board without some help?

Dr J.R. Drummond
Anstruther, Fife

SIR — I do hope F1 bosses will respond positively to the furore about their use of scantily clad pit stop girls.
In the interests of equality they should replace them immediately with honed, toned and tanned chaps wearing skin-tight jeans or shorts and even tighter muscle vests,

speedos (as worn by Daniel Craig), or artistically draped motor stable flags.

Who could possibly object?

Wilma Haley
Doncaster

SIR – I can happily accept the presence of grid girls at motor racing events – I just wish I had been slim enough and pretty enough to be one. What I find very difficult to accept is the waste of good champagne that is sprayed everywhere, and the thought of all that stickiness attracting ants and wasps.

Gill Clark
Wheathampstead, Hertfordshire

Pole position

SIR – I am the proud grandmother of an 11-year-old pole-dancing granddaughter.

It lends a certain frisson to the art of Granny-boasting. If pole-dancing ever becomes an Olympic sport, and the suggestion is that it might, I shall be watching that space.

Veronica Craig
Cavendish, Suffolk

Olympic movement

SIR – Welcome to the "Clare Balding hand/arm waving Olympics". These appear to consist of simulated meat-chopping, garlic-crushing and fly-swatting manoeuvres, interspersed with occasional showings of some of the actual Olympics.

Would it not be possible to handcuff her before we are completely driven to despair?

Michael Beaumont
Turnford, Hertfordshire

SIR – Why is *massive* the adjective of choice by BBC commentators at the Winter Olympics?
The word is being massively overused.

Gordon Casely
Crathes, Kincardineshire

SIR – Describing the results of the British team at the Winter Olympics in terms of "best ever" and "record-breaking" is like saying £10 is a vast improvement on £9.99. I could do better on a tea tray.

Stefan Badham
Portsmouth, Hampshire

Advantage dreamers

SIR – Many years ago I dreamt I was preparing to face Virginia Wade in the women's Wimbledon final. Walking out onto the court I panicked remembering I was (and still am) hopeless at tennis.
Logic then took over and reasoned that if I was in the final I must be pretty competent, and so I stopped worrying.

Maggie Burridge
Axbridge, Somerset

Scream queens

SIR — A friend knocked on the door during Wimbledon. She thought somebody was dying; it was only Maria Sharapova.

> **Brenda Tuppen**
> Storrington, West Sussex

SIR — I am watching the tennis from Eastbourne on the television but I am concerned that I may be guilty of aiding and abetting the BBC in breaking the recent law concerning upskirting. Any advice from your legal team would be much appreciated.

> **John Miles**
> Ely, Cambridgeshire

SIR — Much as I enjoy the skill, tenacity and flair of Rafael Nadal, I do wish someone would advise him to buy a larger pair of shorts and underpants as watching him adjust them before every service is somewhat irritating.

> **Alma MacLeod**
> Newcastle upon Tyne

SIR — Why is the BBC so obsessed with showing slow motion shots during Wimbledon?

While this is sometimes useful to demonstrate the various styles of play, why do we need to see close-ups of the back of players' shoes, and worse still, the drops of sweat coming from Nadal's nose?

> **Bob Kingsland**
> Stroud, Gloucestershire

SIR – It might be opportune to remind television producers at Wimbledon that we don't switch on to see funny hats, or to spot somebody's Mum or girlfriend among the spectators.

Derek Burrows
Liverpool

Royal Mail in a flap

SIR – Royal Mail's management has banned the England flag from their vans during the World Cup.

I'd rather they banned postmen's shorts flying at half-mast.

David Wright
West Malvern, Worcestershire

SIR – In this hot weather, I have discovered a use for the England flags adorning my neighbour's house and car. They are a useful indicator of wind speed and direction, assisting in the prudent opening or otherwise of windows in order to cool down our house.

Ann Garbett
Sheffield

World Wrestling Cup

SIR – I am a fan of wrestling and am delighted that referees now allow the best of wrestling in the Football World Cup.

Brian Birkenhead
London E1

SIR — Is there an orthopaedic specialist who can explain to me how a World Cup footballer writhes in agony after a tap on the ankle but a short while later scores a goal and emerges unscathed from a mobbing by a human pyramid of his team-mates?

George Pearson
Southsea, Hampshire

SIR — Germany has been knocked out of the World Cup.
I believe this is not the first occasion that the Germans have left Russia earlier than expected.

M. Rogers
High Roding, Essex

SIR — In Salisbury a nerve agent to deter the opposition; in Volgograd, in the World Cup, a plague of flies.
Whatever next?

Barrie Taylor
Christchurch, Dorset

SIR — Many thanks for Saturday's headline in the Sport section: "'My team-mates are like brothers to me', says Kane."
I was wondering how to begin Sunday's sermon.

Revd Geoff Richardson
Torquay, Devon

SIR — It appears that wedding guests may abscond because of the football, resulting in a thin attendance. I suggest that vicars use the hymn boards for showing the score. If you can't beat them, join them.

Robin Graham
Broughton, Cambridgeshire

SIR — If anyone would like a ticket to *The Winter's Tale* at the Globe Theatre on the night of the World Cup semi-final, I have a spare one.

My wife will be next to you and will provide congenial company, as long as the conversation does not stray onto difficult topics, such as football or marriage.

David Hipshon
Twickenham, Middlesex

SIR — It's probably just as well England have not reached the World Cup Final.

As I understand it, Theresa May had already agreed to let France win five nil.

David S. Sandhurst
Chaffcombe, Somerset

SIR — How I wish that the World Cup could take place annually instead of every four years. I love the wonderful empty roads every time a significant game takes place.

Janet Newis
Sidcup, Kent

THE ROADS
MUCH
TRAVELLED

Pot luck

SIR – I am perplexed by the constant moaning about the number of potholes on our roads. In my own case it has led to me stepping up my concentration levels to avoid them and thus other road users.

I think the government is to be congratulated on this latest road safety initiative.

R.B. Pugh
Worcester

SIR – As chewing gum so effectively adheres to road surfaces and pavements, could it not be utilised in the repair of potholes?

Tim Watson
St Albans, Hertfordshire

Self-cleaning cars

SIR – Great news that Dyson is producing an electric car. Presumably this will come with various attachments for cleaning?

Fiona Wild
Cheltenham, Gloucestershire

SIR – In the future, when two driverless electric cars meet, headlamp to headlamp, on a single-track road, will the one with the higher-charged battery resort to road rage?

Robert Vickers
Meltham, West Yorkshire

SIR — If electric car charging points are to be installed on our lamp posts, have the authorities considered how many dogs may be electrocuted?

Chris Spurrier
Eversley Cross, Hampshire

SIR — Driverless lorries? I am sure there are thousands of commuters on Southern Rail who would much prefer to see the introduction of driverless trains.

Bruce Chalmers
Goring-by-Sea, West Sussex

Virgin voyage

SIR — I read that Sir Richard Branson is preparing to blast off into space. Will he be returning? These are tremulous moments for the beleaguered passengers on Virgin Trains.

Jo Bird
Slapton, Devon

SIR — Vodafone is to install a mobile network on the moon. A signal in my garden would be nice.

Simon Harris
Falcutt, Northamptonshire

Quiet revenge

SIR — A few years ago, on the whispery commuter train from Salisbury to London, a boorish young man entered the quiet carriage. Manspreading on a corner in the centre of the carriage, he proceeded to make a series of loud and brash business calls.

*Telegraph*s rustled and glances were exchanged with heavy sighs, but nothing happened until the young man received a loud ringing call and the caller was obviously his wife.

At this point a gloriously elegant woman rose from her seat and walked down the aisle, leant over his shoulder and said in a ringing throaty voice: "Darling, why don't you put that silly thing down and come back to bed?"

> **Mandy Peat**
> London SW4

SIR – Packed like sardines on a train from Woking to Waterloo forced me to stand next to a young woman applying makeup. Brushes, lotions and potions were in use, as was what looked like a Dulux colour chart.

The final stage involved something that might have been used during the Spanish Inquisition applied firmly to each eye.

Was it worth it? Not so much. Her face had gone from white-ish to magnolia-ish. And she nearly poked her eye out. But it made the journey more interesting.

> **Eldon Sandys**
> Pyrford, Surrey

SIR – If the gentleman who pushed past me at Waterloo Station on Wednesday is reading this, I would like to inform him that, having tripped over his case on wheels, the pain is now easing and I have managed to get an appointment with the chiropractor.

> **Margaret Scattergood**
> Knowle, West Midlands

Return to vendor

SIR – A farming friend told me of going on a pre-war school visit to London as a child.

There were no hi-vis jackets available but his mother stitched a milk churn label into his jacket, which said: "Return empty to Hazelwood station".

Edward Spalton
Etwall, Derbyshire

Passion wagon

SIR – Your article suggests checking under the seats before taking your car into the garage.

Perhaps you should also check the boot, as my daughter's boyfriend failed to do when his car was towed to a garage following a crash in the Welsh lanes.

He'd left a gross of new condoms littered across the floor of the car boot.

Not only did he fail to mention to the mechanics that he worked in sexual health, he also failed to count the condoms on the car's return.

Judy Parsley
London W4

Grand designs

SIR – I was amused to read about the Daimler that had been buried in a reader's back garden.

This sort of thing was common practice in the 1950s and 1960s when I grew up because people had difficulty in getting rid of unwanted items.

I remember telling my husband that my father had buried a bed, including the mattress, in our back garden.

He replied that his father had buried a grand piano in his grandparents' back garden.

Christine Tomblin
Cotgrave, Nottinghamshire

Road rage

SIR – Perhaps the Manchester police, while endeavouring to catch motorists with mispositioned satnavs, could spare some time to prosecute those who dare to dangle furry dice, mini football boots and other paraphernalia from their rear-view mirrors.

Malcolm Goldie
Hildenborough, Kent

SIR – The trouble with people who drive flashy cars is that they all seem to be driving behind sneering wheels.

Peter Gilbert
Thames Ditton, Surrey

SIR – Autumn is officially here. It's only half-past October and I've just seen my first car with its rear fog light illuminated in bright sunlight in the middle of the day. I'm assuming that it will stay on until April.

Anya Spackman
Watton-at-Stone, Hertfordshire

SIR – When it comes to fake news and misinformation, I would like to nominate the computer which controls the overhead gantries on the M25. It is wrong at least 90 per cent of the time.

Frances Dennett
Epping, Essex

Selfish selfies

SIR – Twice this week I have driven along the A303 past Stonehenge without being delayed by people slowing down to take selfies with the stones – once in the dark and once in thick fog.

This suggests that, instead of replacing the stretch of road with an expensive tunnel, the traffic flow could be improved by erecting a blackout curtain.

Fiona Stevens
Castle Cary, Somerset

You are here

SIR – As an optometrist, I ask my patients if they wear their spectacles for driving. A common answer is: "Only if I'm going somewhere I don't know."

Vivian Bush
Hessle, East Yorkshire

SIR – Yesterday my wife used the satnav system in our car and, as a result, we now measure in kilometres; the settings and language are all in German; and our home has moved from Eastbourne to Crawley.

I would congratulate her if I had any idea where she was.

Mark Rayner
Eastbourne, East Sussex

You say stop

SIR – When I was in South America, an old hand explained the local etiquette at traffic lights: Green means "go" and red means "have a go".

Osmund Stuart Lee
Limpsfield, Surrey

SIR – There's little we should borrow from the French, but alongside better weather and proper wine, their habit of turning traffic lights to flashing amber when traffic is light seems an admirable idea.

Peter Owen
Woolpit, Suffolk

Unwanted litters

SIR – There is an increasing road hazard on our roads. It was once the occasional cyclist, but on weekend mornings, it's now a group of middle-aged people, three riders wide and 20 metres long, all trying to pedal slowly in the most expensive bikes and gear.

I have been trying to work out a plural phrase for this hazard and the best I have thought of so far is "A litter of Lycra".

Mike White
Walsall, Staffordshire

SIR – My wife arrived home yesterday from her regular Friday shop in an unusually happy frame of mind.

It transpired that she had not encountered a single cyclist on the 12-mile round trip.

Roger Wardle
East Horsley, Surrey

SIR – Isn't it about time that we started prosecuting pedestrians?

After all, they make the lives of cyclists a misery by constantly walking on the pavements and getting in their way.

Dave Bassett
Crosby, Lancashire

Cocking a snook

SIR – I once stayed at a bed and breakfast whose address was Court Cocking in St Ives. The landlady was rather pleased with the name but annoyed at the number of times the sign had been stolen.

Peter Boyle
Whitchurch, Shropshire

SIR – I worked for several years next to a company building that surely had one of the worst addresses in the country: Hide, Skin and Fat Ltd, Gas Street, Mumps, Oldham.

Philip Hirst
Ashton-under-Lyne, Lancashire

SIR – Living in Essex, near Chelmsford, I regularly drove past a village called "Howe Green". Its name was proudly displayed on a prominent board. Each time I wanted to stop and add the words: ". . . was my valley".

Fortunately, I resisted the temptation.

Colin McLean
Cley-next-the-Sea, Norfolk

SIR – Walking along the cliffs at Scarborough I noticed one bench facing out to sea, whereas its neighbours all faced inland.

I bent down to read the dedication: "Excuse me, you're blocking the view of my yacht."

I found myself apologising to it, before moving on.

Barbara Mills
Harpenden, Hertfordshire

Bonty Mcbontwyneb

SIR – The Welsh are demanding to choose the name for the second Severn crossing. When the public are allowed to choose new names, something unsuitable is apt to emerge: what's Welsh for Bridgey McBridgeface?

Fiona Wild
Cheltenham, Gloucestershire

SIR – With the rejection of The Prince of Wales as the name for the New Severn Bridge in favour of a person who has done something for Wales, may I suggest Sir Tom Jones.

Freddie Royston
Alton, Hampshire

ROYAL BLUSHES

Fleeing the flight path

SIR – Almost 50 years ago my father was seated next to the Duke of Edinburgh at a luncheon. Making small talk, His Royal Highness asked my father where he lived.

"Windsor, Sir," said my father, "but we are shortly moving to Hampshire to get away from the aircraft noise."

"You are very fortunate," said the Duke. "Sadly, we can't."

Jeremy Spencer-Cooper
Easebourne, West Sussex

SIR – My favourite recollection of the Duke of Edinburgh was after lunch in the Officers' Mess with senior staff at RAF High Wycombe. The mess steward, who was handing out the hats at the door, gave the newest and shiniest, not unnaturally, to HRH.

A recently promoted Air Commodore was left holding the scruffiest. He was last seen running across the car park shouting: "Sir, I think you have my hat."

Stuart Fowler
Cheltenham, Gloucestershire

Family firm

SIR – "Zara Tindall hints at future with Royal Studs", says your headline.

Does Mike know about this?

David Salter
Kew, Surrey

SIR – How wonderful to know that our Queen is expecting again! Another record in her long reign!

Yesterday's *Telegraph*: "Also in attendance was Zara Tindall, pictured curtseying to her grandmother, who is pregnant with her second child."

Dave Bacon
Vale, Guernsey

SIR – Could no one from Help the Aged step forward to prevent a 92-year-old lady being subjected to the two-hour ordeal of the Royal Variety Show?

John Smart
Thornage, Norfolk

Welcome, Prince Dragon

SIR – The new prince, born on St George's Day, cannot be called George as that name is already taken.

Perhaps they could call him Dragon.

Roy Bailey
Great Shefford, Berkshire

SIR – What a pleasant surprise to see an immaculate-looking Duchess of Cambridge leaving hospital so early after giving birth. Presumably they needed the bed and the social worker deemed home conditions suitable for discharge?

Dr Bob Donald
Budleigh Salterton, Devon

SIR — I understand that in Britain during 2017 not a single boy was given the name Ian. I trust that the Duke and Duchess of Cambridge will shortly take steps to restore its popularity.

Ian Burton
Boxmoor, Hertfordshire

SIR — I am always intrigued by the delay in naming a Royal baby: do you think they have been taken by surprise?

Bill Gladstone
Solihull, West Midlands

A child is for life

SIR — My wife and I are amused by all the articles preparing the Duchess of Cambridge to handle the onset of a "Threenager", having survived the "Terrible Twos".

Just to put a perspective on this — and so that Kate doesn't get too complacent — we are now into the "Frustrating Fifties" and still trying to cope.

John Davison
Farnborough, Kent

Unrelated news

SIR — We were astounded to see a photo of a woman called Pippa Middleton on the front page of your paper this morning. I am assuming this is Mrs Matthews, who is of absolutely no interest to us, nor to anyone of our acquaintance.

Patricia Canneva
Epping, Essex

Trooping the colour

SIR – My wife really likes the colourful dresses of the
Duchess of Cambridge.

Perhaps you could find out the charity shop to which she
sends them when she has finished with them.

> **John Mallinson**
> Deal, Kent

SIR – Was the Queen offered any protocol advice on how to
dress when meeting the important Anna Wintour?

> **Charlotte Joseph**
> Lawford, Essex

SIR – I already own the M&S jumper which Ms Markle
has worn and also have the dress your fashion department
is suggesting. As a fast approaching 80-year-old, this has
made my day.

> **Patricia Corbett-Reakes**
> Edinburgh

Sauvez le date

SIR – Knowing how obsessed many of our continental
friends are about our Royal Family, perhaps we could offer
tickets for the forthcoming Royal Wedding ceremony in
return for a preferable trade deal.

> **Gillian Lurie**
> Westgate-on-Sea, Kent

SIR – Should I look out for an invitation to the Royal Wedding or will the modern young couple be sending out what seems to have replaced it – an *invite*?

Bob Shute
Bradford-on-Avon, Wiltshire

SIR – There is an easy way to resolve the problem of the Royal Wedding and the Cup Final being held on the same day. Hold the ceremony in Wembley Stadium, on the hallowed turf, at half time.

Geoffrey Bernstein
Harrow, Middlesex

SIR – It is fortuitous that Prince Harry's fiancée, Meghan Markle, is joining the Royal Family at this time. This means that while the Duchess of Cambridge is on maternity leave, she will have an ideal replacement for her job of going around the country smiling charmingly at people and asking them how they are.

Ted Shorter
Hildenborough, Kent

SIR – Do we know whether the new Duchess of Sussex has ever been to Sussex?

Robert J. Smith
Worcester

SIR – As the government seems to be encountering some difficulty at the moment, perhaps it should consider taking advice from the Royal Family's PR people.

Roy Guy
Harrogate, North Yorkshire

Father of the brides

SIR – As the father of three daughters I can understand why Meghan Markle's father may be having second thoughts about his involvement in the wedding; he has probably become aware of the tradition that the bride's father foots the bill.

K.C. Holt
Horwich, Lancashire

SIR – Meghan's father sounds just the type to carry on the Royal Family's tradition of scandal and should fit in well.

Raymond Bright
West Wick, Somerset

Meghan the feminist

SIR – I see that Meghan is to "fight for feminism".
I would point out that our Head of State is female, our Prime Minister is female, the Head of the Metropolitan Police is female, the Head of the London Fire Brigade is female and the Bishop of London is female.

What chance has a chap got?

Ken Turner
Little Shelford, Cambridgeshire

SIR – When my wife and I were married almost 65 years ago, my bride decided after the formal speeches that she, like Meghan Markle, would like to offer a few words of thanks. As she tried to stand, however, she was impeded by the voluminous skirt of her bridal gown. Being the attentive new husband I moved her chair back a little.

Having had her slightly flustered say, my newly gained wife sat down hurriedly — on the floor. I had moved the chair too far back.

Fortunately only her pride was hurt. As for me, it was simply the first occasion of getting it wrong.

Peter Hindes
Chelmsford, Essex

Crowded aisle

SIR — As I left for the shop my wife Tanya said, "I bet half the country is watching the wedding."

Having got to the supermarket, I discovered where the other half were.

Patrick Smith
Gorleston, Norfolk

SIR — For those of your readers who, somehow, missed the fact during the BBC television coverage of Harry and Meghan's wedding, I can confirm that David and Victoria Beckham were indeed there.

Owen Hay
Stanway, Essex

SIR — While I was attempting to pre-record the Royal Wedding, the caption asked: "record once or the series"?

Are we to expect more than the one marriage for either or both in the future?

Judith Dickinson
Saham Hills, Norfolk

SIR – Eat your heart out, Donald Trump – now *that* was a real mammoth crowd, especially when compared with the vast areas of empty space at the President's inauguration.

> **John Fingleton**
> London W1

SIR – I wonder if the Most Revd Michael Curry should be told the three golden rules of public speaking: be sincere; be brief; be seated.

> **Anne Parmley**
> Blackpool

Standing on ceremony

SIR – Although I wish Harry and Meghan every happiness in their marriage I was relieved that I was not invited to their wedding. I wonder how many reception guests suffer from indigestion if they eat while standing up.

> **Ron Kirby**
> Dorchester, Dorset

SIR – Oh, it's *bowl* food they will be having: and there was me thinking it was *bowel* food. Still, I suppose it comes to the same thing.

> **Bruce Proctor**
> Stonehaven, Aberdeenshire

Organ grinder

SIR – In the Order of Service for that wedding, and in many others across the country year after year, we read that: "The organ will play . . ."

What a clever organ!

Jeremy Thorn (Church Organist)
Fairburn, North Yorkshire

Into the sunset

SIR – Prince Harry has confirmed the old maxim that a man who opens a car door for his wife either has a new car or a new wife.

Dr Dora Henry
Stratford-upon-Avon, Warwickshire

SIR – No more Royal Wedding. Life returns to empty and meaningless normality.

Trelawney Ffrench
London NW3

Common vacancy

SIR – I am thrilled for Prince Charles at his appointment to be the next head of the Commonwealth.

I must admit to being a little disappointed that the post was not advertised; I think I would have made a reasonable candidate, and can be available at short notice for formal dinners and foreign travel.

Lee Smith
Haywards Heath, West Sussex

Narrow escape

SIR – I suppose your reference to "Nuckingham Palace" in today's paper is better than the alternative typo.

Angela Hayes
Wetheral, Cumbria

DEAR
DAILY TELEGRAPH

Dead Tree Media

SIR — The future of *The Daily Telegraph* is in jeopardy: today's published announcements number one birth and 33 deaths. A typical recent ratio.

Darrin Henderson
Tunbridge Wells, Kent

SIR — As a secondary school teacher, I have nine registers to call throughout the week, which represent 254 students. Since qualifying in 1997, I have enjoyed observing the fashionable names that ebb and flow with the times and almost nothing surprises me — until today, when I read in your Announcements that two parents have "produced a son, Ivo, a brother to Compost and Maggot".

V. Thomas
Woking, Surrey

OutRage!

SIR — I was outraged when I saw the picture on page 22 of your paper captioned, "Melanie Rickey, with Mary Portas, left, who she married in 2010".
It should be *whom*. Otherwise, good luck to them.

Roger W.G. Curtis
Presteigne, Powys

You only live once

SIR – As your Obituaries column is often a celebration of lives lived, surely it befits a more uplifting title?

I'll kick suggestions off with "You Only Live Once".

Harry Leeming
Heysham, Lancashire

SIR – I note that nowadays very few people actually "die". In today's paper a proportion of an aquarium's fish were described as having *passed away*. Surely this is a euphemism too far.

Dr Peter Nuttall
Chipping Norton, Oxfordshire

SIR – There have been rather too many recent obituaries of people in their sixties and seventies. It would be of comfort to some of us if you would please print some of more elderly people.

Group Captain Terry Holloway (age 73)
Great Wratting, Suffolk

SIR – If anyone is in any doubt why Britain remains the greatest country on earth, I refer them to the Professor Stephen Hawking and Jim Bowen obituaries, side-by-side in *The Daily Telegraph*.

Barney Schofield
Worsley, Lancashire

From our own correspondent

SIR – I learn today in your paper that Willand is rising by 2cm a year and is "in the middle of nowhere".

Well, yours truly, who is one of your crossword setters, was baptised there in 1945 and went through the village daily in his teenage years, travelling to school from nearby Cullompton to Tiverton. I am delighted to have come from nowhere so as to be able to tell you that nowhere is somewhere.

Don Manley
Oxford

Puzzled readership

SIR – I can't help wondering where your crossword compiler hails from. The only word I can think of to fit in for the clue "seasonal food" is *horseflesh*.

Les Sharp
Hersham, Surrey

SIR – Is the pub quiz featured in the Saturday supplement every week becoming more difficult or am I just getting thicker?

Dr Neil Rhys Thomas
Northwich, Cheshire

Dear Picture Editor

SIR – Freudian slip or intentional pun? The front page of the paper showed a picture of Bryony Gordon in a bra. Below the picture was the word "Features".

Harry Sharp
Bournville, West Midlands

SIR – I find it extraordinary that Poldark's trivial torso should be thrust upon us from the front pages of newspapers.

However, if we are to descend to such banalities, speaking personally I find a man in a suit (ideally three-piece) far more appealing than one so nakedly displayed. After all, there is always the exquisitely tantalising chance that he might remove his jacket.

Suzette Hill
Ledbury, Herefordshire

SIR – From recent events and discussions it is evident that women feel they have been hard done by, but, pause and consider for a moment what a man has to go through to get his photograph on the front page of *The Daily Telegraph*.

John Robinson
Andover, Hampshire

SIR – Why, in every Monday's edition of *The Daily Telegraph*, do we have to have a photograph of Theresa May and her husband leaving church the previous day?

We've got the general idea now.

J.E. Hutt
Leeds

SIR – Are photo editors on a mission to find the most awkward looking facial expressions of our Prime Minister? This seems unkind and even unpatriotic.

Cassandra Hawker
Witchampton, Dorset

SIR – If you must publish disturbing photographs, could you please carry a front-page warning? The picture of Ben Fogle and his wife Marina in front of their bookcase, in which the books were shelved according to the colour of the spines, upset my wife (a librarian) so much that she had to lie in a darkened room for the rest of the day.

Martyn Bedford
Ilkley, West Yorkshire

SIR – Years ago, it was customary to be photographed, cigarette in hand or pipe in mouth.

Now, it is de rigueur to be photographed fondling some mutt or, preferably, three.

How times have changed: not necessarily for the better.

Charles Hopkins
London W10

SIR – Did anyone other than Cate Blanchett attend the Cannes Film Festival?

David Rogers
London SW6

SIR – Seeing your photograph of the actress Daisy Ridley in a "space-inspired black gown" reminded me of a summer's day some 35 years ago when we dressed our seven-year-old daughter in a dustbin bag, stuck on some further items of adornment and entered her into the local Cornish village August bank holiday fancy-dress competition.

She won the top prize.

John Heward
Godalming, Surrey

Dedicated deniers of fashion

SIR – Oh, no: more grim-faced girls dressed by sadists in unwearable clothes. Yes, it's London Fashion Week again. Perhaps next time you could publish a separate fashion supplement. This would make it so much easier to throw it straight into the bin.

Jenny Mowatt
Smarden, Kent

SIR – Hooray! A model on the front page wearing clothes that I, an ordinary 73-year-old, would love to be seen in without appearing I'd lost my marbles. Keep up the good work, Mr Armani.

Jane Avery
Coleford, Gloucestershire

I'm sorry, I'll read that again

SIR – "After ten years of painstaking restoration, Boudicca Fox-Leonard takes an exclusive tour of one of Britain's finest stately homes."

She must look wonderful.

After ten years of that, I think I'd be ready for a day out myself.

M.W.
London SE22

SIR – Not sure how appropriate it was to suggest that the manufacturers of Viagra faced stiff competition.

Robert Mitchell
Poulton-le-Fylde, Lancashire

SIR – I was very impressed to read in the Monday edition, in an article on erosion of coastal defences, that "honeycombed concrete blokes" were installed in the sand dunes as a method of sea defence.

These chaps sound sweet, but are they really up to the task?

Desmond Johnston
Coleraine, County Londonderry, Northern Ireland

SIR – I read that Picasso painted *Le Matador* before he died. Might I enquire as to the paintings he painted after he died?

Roy Endersby
Shirley, Surrey

Breakfast broadside

SIR – I am conflicted. Over breakfast my wife made a throw-away remark that "it's a pity the *Telegraph* isn't printed in tabloid form". And yet I still love her.

Shaun Errington
Macclesfield, Cheshire

SIR – It is with great frustration that I write to tell you that I am spending more time trying to fold your paper than actually reading it. I now understand why butlers were employed to iron papers daily. Could you please consider employing one for me?

Helen Boxall
Dursley, Gloucestershire

Quality newspaper

SIR – I really must congratulate *The Daily Telegraph* on the quality of its paper. Twice this week I have used the local evening paper to light the kindling and have failed, whereas the *Telegraph* has never yet let me down.

John Stevenson
Newport, Shropshire

SIR – Nothing comes close to the *Telegraph* for lining my puppy pens when I have a litter.

Elizabeth Harrington
Higham, Suffolk

SIR — A copy of the *Telegraph* stuffed down the back of trousers proved an effective barrier when the headmaster of my prep school in Scotland was about to administer corporal punishment.

In gratitude, I have been reading the *Telegraph* ever since.

Sandy Pratt
Storrington, West Sussex

Hard sell

SIR — The advertisement in Saturday's newspaper states: "Pensioners snap up new invisible hearing aid."

May I ask: how?

Robert Ward
Loughborough, Leicestershire

SIR — Why do all the advertisements for retirement homes, particularly in your weekend supplements, show happy women with a glass of wine in hand and not a man in sight?

Rich widows?

Dr Paul G. Williams
St Keverne, Cornwall

SIR — We are urged in your paper to "bin the bucket list" — yet on the preceding page there is an advert by a prestigious airline persuading us to "Enjoy more Once-in-a-Lifetimes".

C. J. Wright
Grange-over-Sands, Cumbria

The doctor won't see you yet

SIR – Some years ago, when I was a rural family doctor, I walked into the waiting room and found my next patient reading the *Daily Mail*. I remonstrated with him and suggested that he take both himself and the offending newspaper off the premises. This he duly did and returned shortly with *The Times*.

Despite this, I agreed to see him.

Dr Paddy Fielder
Brandeston, Suffolk

30 years of Matt

SIR – Matt's 30th anniversary has brought back memories of my late father, who for many years was organist at a church in Harrow-on-the-Hill. During the week he would cut out all the Matt cartoons and take them to church on Sunday. The very quiet congregation would be waiting for the service to begin and guffaws of laughter could be heard coming from the vestry.

My embarrassed mother would say in a stage whisper: "Oh, that's your father again, showing his Matt cartoons to the clergy."

Jennifer Russell-Hawkins
Northwood, Middlesex

SIR – Please pass my grateful thanks to Matt for the first wraparound that has not gone straight into the recycling bin.

William Pease
Southam, Warwickshire

SIR – 50 years of reading the *Telegraph*:
8,000 Matt cartoons
10 Prime Ministers
14 General Elections
5 Popes
1 Trump (unfortunately)

Keith Davies
Telford, Shropshire

What's in a name?

SIR – Sophia Money-Coutts; Lady Alice Manners; Boudicca Fox-Leonard.

If I hadn't been sea-fishing with Boudicca I might think these names were made up. Do any Jane Smiths get jobs at the Telegraph?

Richard Mockett
Elsted, West Sussex

SIR – Please put me out of my misery. Is the surname of your feature writer Tom Ough pronounced Ooh, Oh, Ow, Off, Uff or Aw?

Meriel Thurstan
Stoke St Mary, Somerset

Down with this sort of thing

SIR – Tunbridge Wells has been voted one of the happiest
places to live in Britain.

I'm disgusted.

Dr Bertie Dockerill
Shildon, County Durham

Your more humble servant

SIR – You appear to have had a plethora of letters from
Lieutenant Colonels, Wing Commanders, Commanders
RN (retd) of late.

I wonder if anyone can enlighten me – at what level of
seniority is it considered acceptable to use one's ex-military
rank in a signature?

Could I, for example, using my highest rung on the
promotion ladder, sign myself

Your Humble Servant,

Lance Corporal Steven Broomfield (retd)
Fair Oak, Hampshire

Fair hand

SIR – My wife claims she is far too busy to even read the
Telegraph Letters page, let alone find time to write any letters.
I conducted an informal time and motion study on my
wife's activities this morning and am reluctantly inclined to
agree.

Bob Gould
Selsey, West Sussex

SIR — It was wonderful to see so many letters from women in today's Letters page. In order to keep up this progress, please feel free to include this one from me in tomorrow's paper.

Rita Coppillie
Liskeard, Cornwall

SIR — For 30 years I have been in a race with my husband. Who would be first to have a Letter to the Editor published? He won today. Many congratulations or, in the words of the Bard, I scorn you, scurvy companion.

Susan McFadzean
Swansea

SIR — Has anyone ever complained that all letters seem to start with "Sir"?

Richard Hodgkiss
Cheltenham, Gloucestershire

County lines

SIR — As an avid reader of *Daily Telegraph* letters I thought it might be interesting to note over a month their sources.

Unsurprisingly, London came top (42) with Edinburgh (4) and Cardiff (2). The best-represented counties were Surrey (32), Hampshire (28) and Kent (23), followed by Essex, Suffolk and Berkshire clustered around 13.

Humberside was the only English county not represented at least once.

In Scotland, Renfrewshire and Wigtownshire featured

twice, as did Clwyd, Gwent and Gwynedd in Wales. A singleton from Antrim represented Northern Ireland.

Thus the largest numbers were from the Home Counties if one were to include Hampshire and Suffolk.

Although this exercise was just fun for a Dry January, I recall Tom Lehrer introducing his song listing all the chemical elements as potentially being useful "in a somewhat bizarre set of circumstances".

Graham Cooper
Idmiston, Wiltshire

SIR – Has your correspondent Mick Ferrie moved from Mawnan Smith to Falmouth?

I think we should be told. Migration on this scale is a threat to the very fabric of Cornish life.

Hugh Davies
Porthgwarra, Cornwall

The readers have spoken

SIR – Perhaps this year "Letters to the Editor" could be re-named "Still, Small Voices".

Or, in election seasons, "Beware the Fury of a Patient Man".

Graham Clifton
Kingston upon Thames, Surrey

SIR – This week I received, and have read, your latest volume of unpublished letters.

Prior to that I had started to re-read, for the umpteenth time, the earlier books, and am currently on *I Rest My Case* . . .

Three things occur to me. Firstly, the British humour is as eccentric and eclectic as ever.

Secondly, we are still getting hot under the collar about the same subjects. The names of politicians/footballers/celebrities may have changed but the same rants are still there.

Thirdly, and this worries me, there does seem to be a high number of correspondents writing from my county.

Does this mean we are more erudite, or that we ought to go out and get a life?

David Gegg
Ebley, Gloucestershire

SIR — I have just finished reading your latest brilliant compilation of unpublished letters to the *Telegraph*: *Did Anyone Else See That Coming . . .?*

I was somewhat perturbed that there were two significant contributors missing. The first was myself, as it's been a rather unsuccessful year for my letters, I'm afraid.

More worrying was the absence of "M", your Bristol-based asset with his (?) unique ramblings.

Have the Russians got him, or worse yet SPECTRE? Or has he simply run out of one-time pads?

Charles Smith-Jones
Landrake, Cornwall

The last laugh

SIR — *To the folk who publish Telegraph letters*
You obviously think you are my betters.
It seems to me it's purely spite,
When you fail to publish what I write.
Subjects chosen are in the news,
And mine are good, constructive views.
I believe my complaint has just cause,
Yours sincerely, Dennis Dawes.

Dennis Dawes
Winchester

P.S.

Dear Iain,
Thank you for your letter asking if I mind you potentially including one of my letters in *Must I repeat Myself...?* Of course I give my excited, happy permission for you to do so. My Christmas-gifting friend will also be thrilled.

I know you said replies were only necessary in the negative, but golly me, how uncouth.

Every best wish,

Anne Jappie
Cheltenham, Gloucestershire

Dear Mr Hollingshead,
I am delighted to learn that I am to have a letter in your new publication *Must I Repeat Myself...?* You have very kindly published some of my letters in your main paper (43 at the last count) but I have never had one in your *Am I Alone in Thinking...?* series.

I shall ask for it for Christmas.

Best wishes,

Diana Crook
Seaford, East Sussex

Iain,
Thanks for your letter. Most of my letters to the *Telegraph* have been sensible. However, the odd one would even have been rejected by me.

I wouldn't dream of preventing you from using any of them, but since you offer anonymity, I'd quite like to know which one you've chosen, just in case it sounds barking mad a few months later.

Philip Hirst
Ashton-under-Lyne, Lancashire

Thank you for your letter about my letter. Please could you tell me which piece of spluttering outrage you might include? My book is about to be published and my lovely *Guardian* reading agent might disassociate himself with me.

I've read and enjoyed most of your series and given them as presents to other splutterers.

Best wishes,

Jacky King
Castle Cary, Somerset

Mr. Hollingshead,

As I received two letters, does that mean that two letters of mine will be published? Hopefully.

Robert Ward
Loughborough, Leicestershire

THE BEST OF THE
LAST DECADE

Best of British

SIR — At hospital today I was asked to provide proof of citizenship in the form of a utility bill. I really do feel that my wearing of red corduroy trousers, brogues and a tweed jacket should have been sufficient.

Dr Bertie Dockerill
Shildon, County Durham

SIR — When Madonna moved to England she said she wanted to feel more English.

She is shortly to become a single mother with three children from different fathers.

Job done, then.

H.B.
Arkley, Hertfordshire

The slow march of progress

SIR — My first thought on seeing your headline, "Pupils to be taught about sex at seven" was, "What, in the morning?"

When I was a child, the school day began with prayer. But you can't stop progress.

Peter Homer
Highworth, Wiltshire

SIR — I read that Argentina has, at last, legalised same-sex marriages. This pleases me: at this rate of progress, I shall soon be allowed to marry my neighbour's motorbike.

Kevin Hutchinson
Maulden, Bedfordshire

SIR — Gays should be able to marry so they can suffer like the rest of us.

Leslie Watson
Swansea

SIR — I am getting married soon and was completing an email to the registrar outlining, among other things, the music we wish to have played during our ceremony.

My phone helpfully translated *Eine Kleine Nacht Musik* to *Wine Kleenex Nacho Music*. Doesn't that sound like the most tragic night in ever?

Jonathan Oliver
Reigate, Surrey

SIR — Being a devoted husband, as well as a staunch and active member of the Conservative Party, I'd be grateful to learn what further changes it will adopt, especially in regard to monogamy. My wife could do with a bit more help around the house.

Robert Vincent
Wildhern, Hampshire

Till death do us (quickly) part

SIR — I read with dismay the conclusions by university psychologists that men have a shorter life expectancy because they are less likely to seek medical advice.

Married men die before their wives because they want to.

Leonard Gold
London WC2

SIR — I read the advertisements on buses stating that there may not be a God. Obviously these people have not met my wife.

Roy Stainton
Poole, Dorset

SIR — Sir Alan Sugar maintains that making money is better than sex. He obviously has not slept with my wife.

Michael West
Eastleigh, Hampshire

Not this afternoon, darling

SIR — We read with interest the article about having sex every day for 14 days. As I said to my wife, it might do us good to cut down for a while.

Malcolm Holland
Billericay, Essex

SIR — When our family lived in Japan we had a small room within our lounge with obscured glass walls. From time to time our young son was sent there to count to ten and reflect upon his bad behaviour.

Upon our return to the UK the removal men were very keen to know where — and indeed if — they could unpack the box marked "naughty room".

Michelle Bull
London SW19

SIR — Fifty Shades of Grey — succinctly describes my lingerie collection.

Deb Carroll
Stockport

Sex begins at seventy

SIR — Sex after 50, asks your report? I should say so! My partner and I are in our late seventies and still enjoy a stimulating and fulfilling sex life. Long may it continue!

PLEASE DO NOT PRINT MY NAME
Ilfracombe, Devon

SIR — Walking in a Brighton street I was surprised when an elderly lady going in the opposite direction muttered, "You sexy beast." I am 81. It made my day.

Richard Pitcairn-Knowles
Otford, Kent

SIR — A friend of mine, an 80-year-old widow, tells me she receives birth control pills from the NHS as they help her sleep. Curious about this hitherto unknown side effect, I enquired how they work. She said she grinds them up and puts them in her granddaughter's orange juice.

Nicholas Betts-Green
Woodbridge, Suffolk

SIR — I recently received a spam email asking if I wanted to marry "a hot Russian chick". As I'm approaching 75 years of age and have blood pressure problems, I decided on this occasion not to accept this tempting offer.

> **Ivor Yeloff**
> Hethersett, Norfolk

SIR — If I tried balancing my drink on the side of the bath, as suggested by one of your correspondents, I would probably end up with coq au vin.

> **Michael Talamo**
> Carshalton, Surrey

Wham, bang, thank you, son

SIR — I am a 78-year-old widower and wanted some company during my latter years, so I looked at several dating agencies. Not wanting "wham, bam, thank you, ma'am", I decided on the *Telegraph* Dating Service.

I had a couple of dates for which there was no chemistry. The next one, however, was totally different and very exciting. I informed my son of the result. The next time he visited he said, "Dad, I have brought these for you" and handed me two condoms.

I replied to the effect that I had previously undergone a prostate operation and did not require them.

He replied: "Dad, get up to date, you don't need them for that, but in today's world you have to be very wary of STDs."

Later I was working in my garden and suddenly became somewhat peeved that he thought I would require only two when he knew I was away for several days with this younger lady. So I called and asked him why he'd given me only two.

He immediately burst into laughter and replied, "Well, just in case you lost one."

John Ford
Ipswich, Suffolk

PS Please publish this as it makes me laugh every time I think about it, but under a pseudonym, otherwise I will be in deep trouble.

Night riders

SIR — The interest in what parents wear to take children to school reminds me of a friend who, when going to pick up his teenage daughter from a party late at night, always wears his pyjamas.

Pulling up outside the party he attracts the attention of someone coming out and asks if they will go in and tell his daughter that he is waiting outside, adding the rider that if she doesn't come out, straight away, he will come in to collect her.

She appears like the cork out of a bottle.

Peter Smales
Swallowcliffe, Wiltshire

Not feeling lucky

SIR — I've often wondered whether Britain's education system is in a state of decline. Then I visited Google and started to type, "Can I get . . .". Before I finished my query

the first suggested search in the drop-down list appeared:
"Can I get pregnant from a dog?"

Now I know.

> **Robin Whiting**
> Castle Rising, Norfolk

SIR — Thank God prison league tables are being dropped.
I had enough trouble trying to get the kids into decent
schools.

> **Peter Sharp**
> Ascot, Berkshire

Christmas leftover pile

SIR — I have received a lengthy round-robin Christmas
message from someone called Peg. I haven't a clue who she
is, but if she reads the *Telegraph,* could I wish her a rapid
recovery from her recent haemorrhoid operation.

> **Ian McDougle**
> Farnham Common, Buckinghamshire

A bottle a day

SIR — I am now told I can enjoy only 14 units of alcohol a
week. That's fine; I just won't enjoy the rest.

> **Ros Mackay**
> Porthallow, Cornwall

Mood music

SIR – With regards to the "conscious uncoupling" of Gwyneth and Chris Martin, which poor soul is going to be lumbered with that CD collection?

Marlon Zoglowek
Cam, Gloucestershire

DIY spacewalk

SIR – I am a great admirer of Major Tim Peake's achievements – even more so after viewing your front-page photo of him preparing for a spacewalk. Unlike my husband he appears to be reading the instructions before attempting the task.

Marianne Charlesworth
Old Chatton, Norfolk

SIR – Nicola Sturgeon approaches a referendum in a similar style to my doomed DIY projects: keen to instigate and always dissatisfied with the end result.

Paul Coakes
Droitwich, Worcestershire

Private-sector cuts

SIR — I have to admit that I misjudged the strength of feeling by public-sector workers against the cuts — right up to the moment I tried to reduce by 25 per cent the amount of housekeeping money I give to my wife.

Hugh Stewart-Smith
London E11

Marlborough manifesto

SIR — It's good to hear that cigarettes might be sold in plain packets; there will be much more room for government policy to be worked out.

Malcolm Parkin
Kinnesswood, Kinross-shire

Expensive MPs

SIR — May I point out that MPs should be entitled to a fair hearing [with regards to the expenses scandal in 2009], then they should all be shot.

Sheila Shaw
Nelson, Lancashire

Unlike

SIR — I always wanted to be successful and am now pleased to realise that I have achieved this goal. I paid more tax than Facebook last year.

Ed McGrath
Bookham, Surrey

The inglorious eleventh

SIR — People will say I am out of touch, but surely all this rioting and looting [in August 2011] will stop when the perpetrators head for the moors tomorrow for the start of the grouse shooting season?

Nicky Samengo-Turner
Hundon, Suffolk

SIR — I see that the police may be given powers to use water cannon to quell any rioters this summer. If one staged a riot on one's lawn, could one get it watered?

R.W.
Castle Rising, Norfolk

Take that, Tony

SIR — In a calculated snub to Tony Blair, I intend to ignore Peter Mandelson's memoirs before I ignore his.

Gordon Brown
Grassington, North Yorkshire

SIR — Tony Blair stated on the *Today* programme that "he would swap his ten years as Prime Minister for Murray's Wimbledon crown". So would I.

Anthony Gales
Henham, Essex

Bully for Gordon

SIR — Gordon Brown admits to throwing things, but says he has never hit anyone. So it seems that along with all his other failings, he is a rotten shot.

Can the man get nothing right?

Alan Dyer-Perry
North Elmham, Norfolk

SIR — Gordon Brown's smile — could it be wind?

M.H.
Suffolk

SIR — Why, when I contemplate the physical removal of Gordon Brown from 10 Downing Street, am I put in mind of my wife trying to put our cat into its carrier for a trip to the vet?

Ian Bruce
Hockley Heath, West Midlands

The Nick 'n' Dave show

SIR – Am I alone in thinking that Nick and Dave were going to walk away from their first Downing Street press conference holding hands?

John Ward
Ashampstead, Berkshire

SIR – The Dave and Nick partnership appears to be on track. However, if one exchanges the first letter of their names the omens might not bode so well for the future.

Brian Smith
Chelmsford, Essex

SIR –
"I'm bigger than Jesus!"
("Nick" Clegg, after just one TV "Debate")
We've heard that one before:
John Lennon.
And it ended in DISASTER.
A lawful, free and fair election
Requires the "damping down" of any "Boy Cult"
Which seems to have "taken hold".
Because Clegg's "The Future Son-In-Law"
Nobody knows ANYTHING about.
That's all.
cc MI5
Etc.

M

Cold snap

SIR – Mrs May's ill-considered decision to call a snap election merely underlines my deep-seated scepticism of the merits of hiking.

Stephen Wallis
Billericay, Essex

SIR – Much is being written about Theresa May's early life and how she intends to lead the country outside the European Union. But it is an indication of how guarded she is of her opinions that we have no idea which football team she pretends to support.

Mervyn Vallance
Maldon, Essex

Brexit boasts

SIR – I am slightly discombobulated by your statement that the "less educated tended to back Brexit".

Dr Ian Hindle JP PhD MSc BDS FDSRCS FFDRCSI
Scopwick, Lincolnshire

SIR – Slowly but surely the average Englishman has come to an understanding of "smart casual", embracing chinos and linen jackets to great effect. I fear Brexit may put this at risk.

Sue McLellan
London SE26

SIR — I have never thrown an egg at a politician — but I like the idea that one day I might.

In order to protest in this way you need to know who the responsible person is, where you can find them and where there is a good throwing position.

In the EU none of these requirements are satisfied. So I am voting out.

God Save the Queen.

Martin Callingham
London W1

SIR — I have advised my wife that I am to vote Remain in the coming referendum. As she invariably adopts, on principle, the opposite stance to any political or ideological pronouncement of mine, I feel sure I have guaranteed at least two more votes for Brexit.

Pete Matthews
Winchester

SIR — Having changed my mind several times during the EU referendum debate, I now find myself forced to vote Remain as the terms and conditions of the three year guarantee on my new cordless power drill purchased two weeks ago is limited to its use within the European Union.

J.W.
Cortsley, Wiltshire

SIR — It has all been a terrible mistake. We thought that we were voting to leave *Eurovision*.

Dr P.F. Hart
Harleston, Norfolk

SIR – The EU wishes to define the terms for the UK's "divorce" from the EU. Perhaps the EU could take Northern Ireland for a pizza every other weekend.

Hugh Neve
Littlehampton, West Sussex

Special relationship

SIR – I believe that Barack Obama and Jonathan Ross are both 47 years old. There the similarity ends.

Colin Stone
Cellardyke, Fife

SIR – Donald Trump: perhaps best described as "a bull in search of a china shop".

John Stimpson
Clanfield, Hampshire

Nuclear evacuation

SIR – Japan has been holding exercises to prepare for possible conflict with North Korea.

One resident later said: "I was able to stay calm and evacuated in a few minutes."

That's understandable. I'd be fairly nervous too.

Neil Russell
Portsmouth

Striking Libya

SIR – Surely the most effective means of ensuring the no-fly zone in Libya would be to bribe their baggage handlers to strike; it seems to work every summer in Spain.

Anthony Lord
Thornton-Cleveleys, Lancashire

SIR – As Colonel Gaddafi declares an immediate ceasefire in response to the no-fly zone, he once more shows that he is not just a pretty face.

Tom Colborne-Malpas
London SW18

Des ententes cordiales

SIR – The answer to François Hollande's affairs of the heart is that he should abandon the title of First Lady and instead institute First Mistress, Second Mistress and so on.

All of his lady friends would then know where they stand – or lie down.

Ron Mason
East Grinstead, West Sussex

SIR – Could it be said that Sarkozm is the lowest form of twit?

John Thewlis
London SE1

The warm war

SIR — Am I alone in thinking we should tell Vladimir Putin to stick his gas-pipe up his fundament and apply a lighted match to it?

M.E. Martin
Southborough, Kent

Papal indefatigability

SIR — It's Lent, and Benedict XVI has given up being the Pope. I challenge anyone to top that.

Donald Keir
Aberdeen

SIR — *Sede vacante* has not always been connected with the death of a Pope. When I was growing up in the 1970s we would use the expression at home to denote that the bathroom was free.

Andrew Holmes
Bromley, Kent

SIR — The BBC tells us that "the world is stunned" by the resignation of the Pope. I would like to confirm I am mildly surprised at best.

Jonathan Fulford
Bosham, West Sussex

Disappointed reader?

SIR – My favourite – as yet undetected – neologism of the last 20 years is a *fervert* – someone radicalised by any religion.

I know you won't print this, as you never do, but . . . .

Jenny Cobb
Five Ashes, East Sussex

English as she is spoke

SIR – Hats off to head teacher Carol Walker on her attempts to encourage standard English.

In a recent visit to a supermarket in Darlington I overheard the following exchange between a small boy and his father in the sweetie aisle.

Small boy (pointing): "I want them ones."

Father: "No, it's, 'I want them ones, please'."

It's going to be a long struggle.

Brian Jones
Darlington, County Durham

SIR – Having just read the letters about waiters saying "Enjoy", I thought I must tell you that I went into our local cut-price chemists to buy some loo rolls and the young man, as he handed them to me, said, "Enjoy."

I replied: "I'll try."

Graham Upton
Eastbourne, East Sussex

SIR – My wife recently used the expression "from the get go". Is this grounds for divorce?

Andrew Bebbington
Cheadle, Cheshire

SIR – A number of years ago, in a store in California, a dear friend, on taking his receipt from the young, pretty but obviously disaffected sales girl, asked her, "Aren't you going to say, 'Have a nice day'?"
   Her reply: "It says it on the f****** ticket."

Peter Nicholson
Glasgow

Playing the Americans at our own game

SIR – I currently work for a wonderful company run by Americans. However, many of my British colleagues are beginning to find their business vernacular rather annoying: *step up to the plate; came in from left field; ball-park figure; circle the wagons; drink the Kool-Aid.*

We have taken a different approach to combat its pervasiveness: we have invented our own "Empire vernacular", which our American "co-workers" will believe is a quaint old English idiom.

Here are some examples we use regularly: *It's like trying to find the corner on a bowler hat; We can all sip sherry over this one; To hit the driven grouse would mean swinging across the line;* and *I'll stuff the partridge and get back to you.*

Our ultimate hope is that, on global conference calls, we will one day hear these phrases spoken with an American accent.

E.B.
London SW6

Big bush

SIR – Buying a clematis plant recently, my wife and I were reminded that a friend's wife, who often organises charity coffee mornings for lady friends, had on one such occasion been addressed thus by the woman next door:

"Oh, by the way, Thelma, will you ask David to trim your clitoris because it's growing over the top of the party wall?" Is this a record?

> **M.C.M.**
> York

SIR – I cannot tell if Gwyneth Paltrow's latest fad, steaming her vagina, is intended to keep it warm, keep it clean or get the creases out.

> **Kevin Platt**
> Walsall, West Midlands

SIR – Please could the editor explain what he means by extra-martial sex?

> **Dr Wendy Roles**
> Sunningdale, Berkshire

Dave, babe

SIR – I note that, in conversation with her husband, the wife of David Cameron, our most recent ex-Prime Minister, addresses him as "Babe". The winds of change are, indeed, howling more forcefully than I had previously realised.

> **David Salter**
> Kew, Surrey

Ales and Graces

SIR – A friend once ran a pub called the Duke of Hamilton. I called in one morning to find him chortling over a letter he had just received from the local Conservative association. It began, "Your Grace . . ."

He had it framed and hung in the public bar.

Jane Cullinan
Padstow, Cornwall

Dumbed down, BBC

SIR – Once again the BBC failed to do justice to Tolstoy in the final episode of *War and Peace*. Where, pray, was the lengthy second epilogue setting out the author's critique of historiography and philosophy?

"Dumbing down" strikes once more.

John Oxley
London E15

SIR – Am I alone in wishing for an episode of the BBC's *Countryfile* in which a presenter's offer to "lend a hand" is turned down?

Andrew Blake
Shalbourne, Wiltshire

SIR – Christmas was ruined last night by the *Downton Abbey* special. The women were distraught at the demise of Matthew Crawley, while the men were more concerned about the possibly irreparable damage to his car.

Cynthia Dunn
Rhosllanerchrugog, Wrexham

Blind corner

SIR – I don't give up my seat for the blind.

Twenty years ago a blind woman entered my Tube carriage. She had dark glasses, a white stick, a dog – the full kit. I naturally offered her my seat, only to be berated: "I may be blind but there's nothing wrong with my legs."

She continued to make remarks the whole journey, much to my embarrassment and the sniggering amusement of fellow commuters behind their papers.

Eventually I reached my stop and sprinted off, only to realise when I got to work that I had left my briefcase behind. On calling London Underground I was informed that a suspect briefcase had indeed been found, the District Line suspended and the Bomb Squad called to Bow Road.

Upon eventually arriving at Bow Road by taxi ("It'll take a while, Guv'nor, Mile End Road's chocker. Bomb at Bow Road.") I was immediately marched to the station manager ("Yes, that's my briefcase. Yes, that's right, the one with *The Lover's Guide* video in it.")

Humiliation over? Oh no. Upon getting the crowded Tube back to the City, a ticket inspector got on. Naturally I hadn't bought a ticket when being marched down to see the station manager at Bow Road. I then had to explain in front of everyone why I was travelling without a ticket.

I can still vividly recall the face of the woman who screamed: "I'm late for an interview because of you."

Now I don't even like people in sunglasses.

H.A.
Hambledon, Surrey

Cattle class

SIR – The EU states that a small calf transported by rail must be afforded a space of between 0.3 metres and 0.4 metres squared in which to travel.

I was wondering to whom I should write to complain about the fact that my feet didn't touch the floor for 45 minutes on the 17:44 to Sevenoaks from London Bridge last night.

S.B.
Sevenoaks, Kent

Invasive security

SIR – I find it intensely humiliating to be asked by airport security staff if I have packed my own bag. This forces one to admit, usually within earshot of others, that I no longer have a manservant to do the chore for me.

Gentlemen should be able to answer such questions with a disdainful: "Of course not! Do I look like that sort of person?"

Arthur W.J.G. Ord-Hume
Guildford, Surrey

SIR – It is a pity Osama bin Laden was not taken alive. He could have been sentenced to go through airport security for the rest of his life.

Sandy Pratt
Lingfield, Surrey

Inflexible speed limits

SIR – Why do all speed limits on our roads end with a zero (20, 30, 40 etc.)? Such a lack of flexibility and imagination by those who wish to control us.

Bruce Pearson
Godalming, Surrey

Kings, Queens and Jokers

SIR – Am I alone in noticing that the Queen looks far happier on the front page of the *Telegraph* than in the *Guardian*? Is she trying to tell us something?

Fred Ford
Salford

SIR – In defence of Prince Harry [who in 2009 used the word 'Paki' to describe a member of his platoon] I have to say that after 30 years residency in this country I trust people a lot more who call me a "f----- German bastard" to my face than those who hide their prejudices behind a veneer of discreet bourgeois politeness.

Reiner Luyken
Achiltibuie, Ross-shire

SIR – Now that Prince Charles is entitled to a free bus pass I do hope that he does not bring too many minders with him when he travels on the 195 from Great Hollands to Bracknell Bus station. It sometimes gets rather crowded.

Revd Michael Bentley
Bracknell, Berkshire

SIR — While I very much enjoyed the Royal Wedding, I did miss the BBC failing to interview William and Kate on their way back down the aisle asking, "How does it feel?"

> **Bruce Ridge**
> Cleveden, Somerset

SIR — While I was browsing the article by Judith Woods on the posterior of a certain bridesmaid, a young lady gracefully swayed past. A young man within earshot commented, "What a lovely 'Pippa' she has." Has a new word entered our lexicon?

> **Ted Forsyth**
> Guildford, Surrey

SIR — All these years I have lived under the impression that Middleton Bottom was a rural West-Country village.

> **Keith White**
> Conford, Hampshire

SIR — Why does your newspaper make such a fuss about Pippa Middleton? I see better-looking girls in the queue for Greggs in Walsall.

> **Kevin Platt**
> Walsall, West Midlands

SIR – When Prince William married Ms Middleton, the comparisons made implied that he was marrying his mother. Now, according to the nauseating drivel on your front page this morning, he seems to have fathered his mother. This is beyond Oedipus.

Jane Bonner
Pudsey, West Yorkshire

SIR – Two days of news about the Duchess of Cambridge, and you haven't yet told us about her hospital gown. Who designed it? How much did it cost? And has she worn it before?

J.S. Hillmore
London N20

SIR – I have a soft spot for Sarah Ferguson; my dream girl looked like her and she reminds me of a boisterous Labrador, my favourite breed of dog.

Mark Taha
London SE26

Reverse sledging

SIR – Forget reverse swing. Has the England cricket team considered the tactic of reverse sledging during the Ashes series? Example: "I say, my wife tells me you're awfully good in bed."

Robert Solomon
London NW3

Wayne's world

SIR – I don't know who scares me more when they're in full verbal flow: Wayne Rooney or Colonel Gaddafi.

Ivor Yeloff
Hethersett, Norfolk

Supermarket sweep

SIR – Was losing 2-1 to Iceland really such a terrible result for English football? We could have lost by a huge margin if we had played Sainsbury's or Tesco.

Leonard Clark
Bristol

Lady Ziegler's Lover

SIR – I was watching the ladies tennis match between Sharapova and De Brito, complete with agonised, competitive caterwauling. Through the open garden door, looking unusually sheepish, stepped our gardener. He confessed later that he'd been most relieved to see the green grass of Wimbledon on our screen. From his position amongst the roses he was convinced that Mrs Z and I were watching a porn film.

Zog Ziegler
Haw Bridge, Gloucestershire

SIR – Overheard outside one of the gates onto Centre Court at Wimbledon: "Now, do you need the loo before we find our seats?"

"Mum, I'm 51."

Jo Marchington
Ashtead, Surrey

Tom Daley, CIA double

SIR –

"Tom" Daley.

"14-year-old".

"Genius Diver".

Looks like he MAY be a CIA "Double".

Though the "Double" MAY be Canadian.

Probably 17 years old.

Look at page 55 of the "Sport" section.

And THINK "Jim Carrey".

The mother?

MOTIVE?

Probably MONEY.

cc The British State

"MI5"

GCHQ

22 SAS

"MI6"

FCO

M

The third coming

SIR – Your headline in the Sport pages, "Jesus fit again" reminds me of when, in the 1960s, Liverpool Football Club fielded a legendary forward line, including Arrowsmith, St John and Callaghan.

An evangelistic slogan had been painted in large white letters on a block of grim Liverpool Council flats: "What will ye do when Christ cometh to Liverpool?"

Below someone had added: "Move St John to midfield".

Nick Marler
Otley, West Yorkshire

Dear Picture Editor

SIR – Setting aside the morality issues, let's at least relish the opportunity Berlusconi's bunga bunga activities have provided *Telegraph* picture editors to adorn the newspaper with some cracking crumpet.

David Creffield
Lancing, West Sussex

Battle of the sexes

SIR – Since you reported the impending opening of a lap dancing club here in Henley-on-Thames I have organised new glasses and a blood pressure check with my doctor. I can't wait.

Robert Warner
Aston, Oxfordshire

SIR — Please stop publishing letters from my husband, Robert: after three in less than a fortnight, he is insufferable and has now taken to reading the Letters page online at 2am in order to get his oar in first.

Enough is enough, especially as there are still lawns to mow, leaves to sweep and logs to split.

Anne Warner
Aston, Oxfordshire

SIR — Apart from a boyish desire to show off, men write to newspapers to make up for their inability to communicate normally.

David Miller
Tunbridge Wells, Kent

Veteran wags

SIR — As I read in the obituaries the fascinating story of yet another war-time hero who has sadly passed away, I wonder if, in 50 years time, all your future readers will have to read about are the exploits of *Big Brother* contestants and WAGs?

Jane Bryan
Devizes, Wiltshire

PS

SIR — What do 100 "academics" actually do when they're not writing to *The Daily Telegraph*?

Jasper Archer
Stapleford, Wiltshire

SIR — The letters books are a great source of amusement, but I had to remove them from my downstairs loo as guests were of the same opinion. I wondered why they remained in situ for so long, and I have now had to banish the books to the upstairs loo.

Margaret Wilson
Hungerford, Berkshire

SIR — Forget the front page and all the pages in between, I always turn straight to the Letters, where I know I will find enlightenment, amusement and teeth-grinding irritation. Pity it is so short.

John Pearson
Hove, East Sussex

SIR — As a regular visitor to the UK, I have been fascinated by the spate of letters regarding the television viewing of assorted pets. They have reinforced my view that the British are quite, quite mad.

Long may it be so.

John Eagle
Norwich